ue

D1159884

WHITE MAMMOTHS

ALEXANDER POLIAKOV *has also written*
RUSSIANS DON'T SURRENDER
translated by NORBERT GUTERMAN

"It happens to be my task to read a mass of books coming out on various problems of the war. I shall rank this among the very finest that have appeared in the last few years. It can have a notable effect, not merely on American thinking, but it summons and fortifies those deeper emotions which are essential to victory."

ARTHUR UPHAM POPE

"To understand the spirit behind the heroic resistance of the Russian Army to the German onslaught, and to get a vivid picture of personal courage, sacrifice, suffering and devotion of the Russian masses to the cause of freedom, one should read Alexander Poliakov's book."

DR. TARAKNATH DAS

"I know of no other book on present-day Russia so clear in its presentation, and so effectively told, as *Russians Don't Surrender*. It illustrated the simple, undeviating determination of the whole Soviet population to drive the enemy from the beloved soil."

REBECCA JANNEY TIMBRES

"This stirring story of indomitable courage, incredible ingenuity, and of will to conquer should be placed in every library in the land."

JOHN A. KINGSBURY

"It sounds a note of triumph that cannot fail to be an inspiration to us in America and to the English. Poliakov has penned a narrative that makes one sure of the victory of the brave Russian people. The pictures are fascinating. You are rendering real service through its publication."

WILLIAM JAY SCHIEFFELIN

"The spirit of the entire fighting and civilian population is evidenced, but also the ingenuity, cunning and unfailing humor. The book contains some grand yarns. Ungarnished, unaffected, this book has the pace and excitement of fiction and the mark of authenticity."

VIRGINIA KIRKUS

"Poliakov's *Russians Don't Surrender* is more than literature. It is also more than just a human document. It is the voice of the Soviet's Unknown Soldier on the vast steppes of Russia, fighting stubbornly against Hitler's perfectly equipped bandits and battling exultantly for his national freedom. . . . This simple war diary reflects their spirit, faith and determination. . . . It cannot fail to inspire its readers."

PIERRE VAN PAASSEN,
from the Introduction to *Russians Don't Surrender*

Published by E. P. DUTTON & CO., INC.

WHITE MAMMOTHS

The Dramatic Story of
Russian Tanks in Action

By

ALEXANDER POLIAKOV

Translated from the Russian by
NORBERT GUTERMAN

Illustrated with Photographs

New York · 1943
E. P. DUTTON & CO., INC.

AMERICAN BOOK—STRATFORD PRESS, INC., NEW YORK

CONTENTS

CHAPTER I
An Evacuated Factory
page 11

CHAPTER II
Tank Instruction Centre
page 20

CHAPTER III
Train to the Front
page 27

CHAPTER IV
Science at the Front
page 38

CHAPTER V
New Year's Eve
page 52

CHAPTER VI
The March Over the Ice
page 68

CHAPTER VII
First Battles, First Trophies
page 83

CHAPTER VIII
The Mammoths Attack
page 93

5

CONTENTS

CHAPTER IX

The Death of Commissar Kharchenko
page 106

CHAPTER X

Forty-Eight Hours in a Besieged Tank
page 115

CHAPTER XI

Forward Under the Soviet Flag
page 122

CHAPTER XII

A Heroic Name
page 128

CHAPTER XIII

Staraya Russa
page 132

CHAPTER XIV

Conversations Man to Man
page 142

CHAPTER XV

Tanks Against Tanks
page 151

CHAPTER XVI

"Trophy" and the Loss of No. 512
page 163

CHAPTER XVII

The School of Courage
page 177

LIST OF ILLUSTRATIONS

Facing page

Reconnaissance on the snowbound Russian front	16
Factory workers in a Urals plant assembling tanks	17
Women electricians checking a tank	17
A huge tank is hoisted into place inside the factory	32
Completed KV's and their crews	32
The massive trees cracked under the caterpillars	33
They had to climb the steep snow-covered bank	33
Everywhere local residents with their families follow close behind advancing Red Army	36
Residents makes temporary homes in dugouts	36
A woman collective farmer returns home to ruins	37
Several families take refuge in a single dugout	37
Residents eagerly return to their villages	44
A Russian soldier finds everything destroyed but the chimney	44
Homeless Russians find shelter in German dugouts	45
Russian children whose parents were taken prisoner	45
Russian women weep for their dead	48
A mother without family or home	48
Russian soldiers celebrate New Year's at the front	49
A New Year's party in the traditional way	49
Tankmen checking their arms before an attack	64
Tanks deploying for action	64
New tanks heading toward advanced lines	65
Russian tankists receiving final battle instructions	65
Taking the oath prior to an engagement	68
A tank-borne infantry detachment rolls into battle	68
Infantry attacking under cover of tanks	69
Infantry and tanks storm the enemy	69
Red Army men taking German soldiers prisoner	76
Tankmen escorting German war prisoners	76

7

LIST OF ILLUSTRATIONS

Facing page

War-weary women and children 77
Young brothers wounded by the Germans 77
Children shot by the Hitlerites 80
A baby with its mother killed by the Germans 80
Camouflaged sleigh-borne troops prepare 81
Red Army men advancing toward the enemy under cover
    of a tank 81
A tank-borne detachment on a fighting operation 96
Camouflaged infantry are carried behind tanks 96
A tank-borne detachment mounting the tanks 97
Russian tank and camouflaged troops 97
Peaceful citizens in a shallow trench   *between pages* 120-121
Women removing bodies of relatives shot by the Germans
                          between pages 120-121
Russian men and boys murdered by the Germans
                          between pages 120-121
Russian residents welcome their Soviet liberators
                          between pages 120-121
Russian families seeking their dead   *between pages* 120-121
Wholesale killing of Soviet citizens   *between pages* 120-121
A bereaved father bends over the bodies of his wife, son
    and daughter   *between pages* 120-121
KV tank field repairs at the front 144
A hero greeting a group of young satellites 144
A duel between a Russian and a German tank 145
Russian tank camouflaged with hay and snow 145
Russian troops return to their ambushed tank 160
Alighting from tanks in the theatre of war 160
A tank-borne infantry detachment boarding the tanks 161
"To achieve final victory we must eliminate their
    superiority." 161
The indomitable Russian people return to their villages 180
A liberated farmer and his family 180
Automatic riflemen going into battle against the Nazis 181
Repairing KV tanks at the front 181
New KV tanks 188
Camouflaged tanks speeding to the front 189

8

WHITE MAMMOTHS

Chapter I

AN EVACUATED FACTORY

THE FACTORY seems endless, its buildings stretch for miles and miles and its smoke belches from hundreds of chimneys. A deafening mechanical roar fills the air—the throbbing pulse of this industrial Hercules, created by the Five Year Plan. The factory knows no rest, no fatigue. The workers take no days off, observe no holidays. They are like front line soldiers: they do not simply work, they fight, like the whole of our country, like all of our people.

Recently evacuated from Leningrad, this factory —the Kirov Works—has been installed on the site of a Ural plant, far behind the lines. Some of the workers remained in their native city, but several thousands were flown here to make the most powerful tanks in the world for the Red Army.

The energy and quiet determination of the new-

11

comers soon became the talk of the entire district. "The front must get as many tanks as it needs," they declared to their fellow workers of the Ural. What the Ural factories produced at the beginning of the war was no longer sufficient, and no one realized this better than the workers from Leningrad who had frequently worked under enemy fire.

Orders for materials were sent to every corner of the Urals. The gigantic Magnitogorsk plant was harnessed to the task. Production figures of pig iron, steel smeltings and finished armor plate began to climb. Orders from the transplanted Kirov Works were considered like orders from the Fatherland itself.

On the first day of my visit I met small groups of foremen and workers who had come to the factory from the tank delivery department, which is responsible for the final assembly, adjustment, trial run and delivery of the finished tanks to the Red Army. From this department the tanks roll down the cement incline to the freight cars which take them to the front.

"Why are you here?" I asked one of the foremen, a middle-aged worker. "Have you come to pay us a visit?"

12

"The other departments are lagging behind us," he replied indignantly. "They're lagging behind us, and we're lagging behind the front. We've got to put some pep into them. That's the kind of visit we're making."

In one department the shock brigade walked straight into the workers' general meeting and made the laggards feel ashamed of themselves. In another, they lent a hand to the workers. The day after this "raid," tank production showed a considerable spurt forward.

The assembly and delivery department is the most impressive of the new additions to the plant. Long trains loaded with parts ready for assemblage roll ceaselessly into its huge lofts; powerful stationary cranes are suspended from its high ceiling; mobile cranes slowly nose their way along the tracks. Swaying gently in the air, they safely convey the skeletons of future tanks weighing several tons each, and turrets, guns and motors to their various destinations. The parts are assembled and tested amid the din of welding and riveting. The tank is then picked up as if it were an infant by the factory's most powerful crane, and the girls cover it with a nice layer of snow-white paint. Testers drive the

13

new-born tank to the tankdrome, run it at high speed, make it spin around like a whirligig, take it over obstacles and drive it down into pits while its guns and machine guns are tested on the shooting grounds.

Alexei Volkov, a veteran Putilov worker, is in charge of the delivery department. He is a man of small stature and slender build with vivacious clear gray eyes. He wears several decorations, among them the Order of Lenin recently awarded him for exact fulfilment of important war orders. He has been employed in the production of tanks for eleven years, and assembled the first tank of the KV (Klementi Voroshilov) type. In the winter of 1939, when the KV tanks went into action against Finland, Alexei Volkov and his squad of assistants went to the front. Ignatyev, Kovsh and Kolkov were at the wheel during the fighting; Istratov and Volkov himself effected the necessary repairs in the heat of battle. Now these five men, all decorated for their outstanding service, work in Volkov's shop.

The workers' discipline and devotion are admirable. In the assembly department the work must be done with particular care; one tiny error here can nullify the efforts of thousands of workers. Volkov

14

does not mince words when he discovers defective work. "Are you working for the Germans?" he once asked a young worker who had made a mistake. The boy nearly burst into tears. "I'd rather have you take it out of my pay, Alexei Semyonovich," he said. "I'll work a whole day for nothing. But don't say such things; they kill me." Volkov let him off with the strict injunction "not to turn out any more junk."

The whole spirit of the factory reminds you of the front. The workers were brought here like air-borne troops, and they are fully aware of the military importance of their work. They are at their machines from twelve to sixteen hours a day. People like Volkov and his assistants have hardly left the factory grounds for months at a stretch.

* * *

Recently Marshal Klementi Voroshilov visited the plant. When he arrived at the Assembly Department he was immediately surrounded by a throng of workers who showered him with questions:

"How are things going at the front?"

"What's the news from Leningrad?"

A finished KV tank became his platform. The first

15

Marshal of the Red Army had once been a Lugansk mechanic, and now he climbed up on one of the machines named in his honor to address the men of his former trade. He spoke amid a hushed silence:

"Comrades, Stalin says that to achieve final victory over the Germans we must eliminate their superiority in tanks and planes. This means that victory is up to you, that it is within your power to bring closer the hour of reckoning with the enemy. Stalin asked me to tell you that the front expects more and more of the splendid tanks you are making."

Amid roars of laughter and outbursts of cheering Voroshilov proceeded to tell how terror-stricken the Nazis were at the sight of our KV's. "The Nazis call them Soviet Mammoths," he said. "Let us have more of them. Let them sharpen their tusks on the Nazi scum, let them uproot those vermin and hurl them out of the land of the Soviets."

An interesting incident took place in the engine department. Walking down one of the aisles between the lathes, Voroshilov stopped near an old foreman. Dressed in blue overalls with gauges protruding from his enormous pockets, the man stood out among all the others because of his stern expression and his black moustache.

16

Reconnaissance on the snowbound Russian front. (*Sovfoto*)

Factory workers in a Urals plant assembling Russian tanks for front line defense. (Sovfoto)

Women electricians checking the wiring of a tank before it leaves the plant. (Sovfoto)

"Hello, friend," said Voroshilov. "Aren't you Khudyakov?"

"That's me all right, Klementi Yefremovich."

"Those are some whiskers you've got there! What are you doing here?"

"Making engines as you see. We've been evacuated."

More than twenty years ago Khudyakov had fought as a partisan under Voroshilov. Now the foreman and the Marshal recalled how they once succeeded in shooting their way out of a circle of White Guards.

"Well, it's war again and everyone must do his utmost," said Voroshilov.

"That suits me fine," said the foreman, "but I wish I were at the front."

"Drop that talk. Haven't you got a front right here?"

"Sure, but I'm itching to get my hands on those damned Nazis."

"There are younger men than you for that. You probably have someone at the front yourself."

"Of course, my son Vassili."

"What is he doing?"

"A tankman on a KV."

"Then what are you kicking about, old whiskers? The father is making tanks and the son is fighting in them. You're a grand old fellow, that's sure!"

* * *

On one of the machines in the polishing department I noticed a small red flag with the inscription "For Stakhanovite Work." A round-faced young woman with a three-cornered red kerchief around her head was the operator. Anna Martyanova was a local Stakhanovite who had surpassed normal production schedules four times and earned nine hundred rubles a month. When I went to see her during a rest period she was in a happy mood. "Yesterday I received a letter from my husband," she exclaimed joyfully. "I had not heard from him for over three months. He writes that his regiment has been awarded the Banner of the Guard Troops. We in our department are going to receive the honorary Red Banner by the end of the month. You see, we, too, are Guardsmen."

A friend of Martyanova's, Vera Kurdyuk, who works on the same shift, was recently informed that her husband, a lieutenant, had been killed in action. Despite her grief, she has not lessened her efforts.

18

She is still a Stakhanovite. More and more tank parts! More and more Soviet Mammoths! This is the best method of avenging her husband's death.

The ties between the factory and the front are ties of blood. It is true that working conditions are hard, that for a long time now the workers have not been to a theatre, have not heard a concert except over the radio, have not seen a moving picture. But how happy they are when upon leaving the factory they see a long line of finished tanks, their own handiwork, being driven off to the testing ground! The mere sight of these mobile fortresses compensates them for all their wartime hardships.

Chapter II

TANK INSTRUCTION CENTRE

When a tank has passed every test and is ready for delivery, a carefully trained crew takes charge of it. It is of great importance that the crews receive part of their training at the factory itself, and whenever possible, on the very machines which they will take into battle. For this reason, the proving grounds are situated close to the plant.

Ten days before leaving for the front, the crews are attached to their respective "boxes," as the armor-plated chassis of their future land battleships are called. From that moment on, the crew and the tank form one living unit. The commander of the machine, the driver-mechanic, the gunner, the repair man and radio operator join the workers in the assembly department. The tank is put on rollers and is equipped with caterpillar treads and a bristling row of cannon and machine guns. Inside, the motor, the transmission, the radio set, the optical instruments and a thousand smaller items are installed. As the days pass, the steel fortress becomes increasingly alive. Soon the powerful motor begins to hum, the electric headlights blink, the horn blares.

I saw a group of powerful KV tanks rolling toward the exit. They were commanded by Lieutenant Astakhov, a tall, well set-up boy of twenty-three with a long determined face and a suggestion of a smile in his eyes. He had already seen action as the commander of a unit. He had been wounded and was now about to return to the front.

I had watched his crews for several days as they went about the endless painstaking task of assembling their tanks with the help of the workers. The crew was no longer greasy and grimy. They were neat and clean and they wore new overalls, for they were going out for the final test. The tank plant is the first of the classrooms of the Tank Centre. The artillery ground is the second, the tankdrome the third, and the fourth and final grade is on an open field interspersed with woods, which is used for tactical instruction. Here there are no classes confined within four walls, with a ceiling, a blackboard and a bell to announce recess. The instruction is not based on colored illustrations of tanks, but on real tanks and tank parts. Most important, the trainees at the Tank Centre are carefully selected from people familiar with machines. Not so long ago the men forming the crews were combine operators, tractor drivers or chauffeurs.

Military Engineer Novotortsev was in charge of training at the Tank Centre. He and Major Shevazudsky, artillery instructor, were inseparable.

"Today, Fedor Petrovich, we'll be partners," said Novotortsev to Shevazudsky as they sat down to breakfast.

"Yes. We'll watch your drivers bump into houses on their way to the firing ground," taunted the major.

"Not on your life, Major," retorted Novotortsev. "But we will see your gunners blazing away at everything but their targets. It'll be pleasant to watch them."

The commanders' breakfast passed quickly and pleasantly amid jokes about the impending "partnership exercises," which in tank instructors' language means combined exercises involving shooting and driving.

* * *

The five KV's with Astakhov in the leading tank headed for the tankdrome. The other four tanks were commanded by Lieutenants Chilikin, Kalinichev and Yefimov and Second Lieutenant Gomozov. It was a clear winter morning. The dazzling white snow in the bright sun blinded the eye. The forty-five degree frost pinched the skin. But once inside their machines the tankmen do not fear the cold. The motor gives off heat continually, the guns are constantly ready to discharge more heat and the men themselves are warm with patriotic ardor.

The huge steel mammoths roared down the main street past the factory, shaking the buildings and pressing heavily on the snow. Without hitting a single corner they arrived safely at the training grounds. These were intersected by several ditches, a rivulet and a small oak woods. A string of slightly projecting spars outlined the anti-tank obstacles under the deep snow. Captain Glushkov, together with the two instructors, gave Astakhov the following tactical assignment: "Carry out a frontal attack on the enemy's strongly fortified defense line and overwhelm his tanks and artillery with your fire and caterpillars."

The tanks dashed forward. The massive spars

23

cracked under the caterpillars like lumps of sugar under the impact of a strong set of teeth. Nor did the anti-tank pits stop the machines. Next they had to climb up the steep snow-covered bank of a ditch. All five machines succeeded in getting through the waterway and made a dash for the opposite bank, but one after another they began to slip back on the frozen surface of the incline or to spin helplessly around. A few more thrusts proved futile. The attack failed.

"And you call yourselves tankmen? And with tanks like the KV's, too?" bawled Novotortsev indignantly. With an abrupt gesture he ordered his men to leave the tanks. "And you call yourselves mechanics," he shouted turning to the drivers. "You act as though you were leading a dog on a leash, not driving a tank."

The crews stood silent with downcast eyes, throwing side glances at that accursed bank. They had failed to scale it because they expected it to be soft as in summer, rather than hard as granite as it was now.

"I'll drive one myself," said Novotortsev and he climbed into the nearest tank.

The machine started. The tank crews watched the

engineer drive twice along the side of the ditch to gather speed, then resolutely dash across. On the opposite side, the tank at first skidded and spun around, as though made dizzy by the steep climb, and even began to slide back. Then it made a few sharp turns and by bold zigzagging soon negotiated the hill. Once on top, the engineer emerged shouting something and pointing with his right hand at the course he had taken. Then he resumed his seat and returned saying that he would now demonstrate another method of taking a steep slope at high speed. "Look, there are some bushes and trees. You thought they would prove an impassable obstacle. You have not yet realized the power of your machines." Steering straight for the copse he dashed forward with such impetuosity that before I realized what was happening the tank uprooted a tree which crashed across the machine leaving a gaping crater. Utilizing the traction of this crater the tank quickly climbed up the slope.

In the course of the following hour all the tanks repeated Novotortsev's performance.

The marksmanship of the gunners was tested at night. Major Shevazudsky at first grumbled because Novotortsev had prolonged the driving tests, but he was finally mollified. Night shooting is a real science, and is extremely important at the front. The artillery men and machine gunners passed their tests with flying colors, making several direct hits. This was no surprise: four out of the five crews had seen actual fighting in this war.

Tatyana Mikhailovna Frunze, daughter of the famous general who was one of the founders of the Red Army, worked as a technician in the factory's laboratory. She accompanied us to the testing grounds. She is very friendly with the tankmen, and each successful manoeuvre aroused her admiration. The tankmen loved to see her standing there and were proud of displaying their skill in her presence.

Later at night the crews returned to their battalion, and after a hot dinner went to the Lenin Corner to chat or read magazines. On the wall newspaper I noticed several clippings neatly arranged. They described the heroic exploits of a certain KV tank crew who in their first battle destroyed seventeen enemy guns, several dozen pillboxes and a hundred riflemen. "They're from our battalion," Senior Political Instructor Lukasz said with pride. "We're trying to make all our soldiers as efficient as those boys."

Chapter III

TRAIN TO THE FRONT

O̲ur o̲ld acquaintances, the five KV tanks, cautiously crawled up into huge platform cars. The engine was already warmed up and the crews lined up beside the train. Facing the crews was a line of workers and engineers from the factory including shop representatives and heads of the labor brigades which had assembled, tested and driven the tanks. Everyone who had had a hand in creating the giant fortresses had come to see them off. There was the manager of the factory, engaged in lively conversation with the chief of the Tank Instruction Centre; there was old Khudyakov contentedly stroking his luxuriant moustache; there was Tatyana Frunze, a trim and erect little military figure with a constant smile on her lips; there were Engineer Novotortsev, Major Shevazudsky and many others.

27

In a simple and moving ceremony, the workers' representatives "handed" the tanks over to the soldiers who were to man them. "After having tested it, I hereby deliver to you this tank made in our factory; it is in perfect fighting condition," declared the senior brigade leader, who was later awarded a decoration for his good work. "I hereby accept this tank in perfect fighting condition," said Lieutenant Astakhov, commander of the first machine and of the whole unit, as he "received" his tank.

After the presentation of the other four tanks, the factory manager made a short address to the tankmen. "Use these tanks," he said, "to ram and crush and shoot to hell the vile Nazi vermin. Free our cities and villages, and secure our complete victory. And give the Germans a double dose when you get near our beloved Leningrad."

Then the factory manager and the commander of the tank unit cordially embraced, pledging themselves to fight to the finish. Their gesture seemed to symbolize the deep indissoluble unity of workers and soldiers.

After the official ceremonies, came the general leave-taking from friends and relatives. Lieutenant Astakhov walked over to his wife who had been standing modestly at some distance. He had introduced me to her the previous evening. This recent graduate of a nurses' training school was a well-formed young woman, with a dark complexion, candid hazel brown eyes, full but beautifully drawn lips, and dark locks curling from under her white beret. The young couple had been married only a year and a half.

Standing by the train that was to carry her husband off to the front Lena was unable to refrain from tears when Astakhov tenderly placed his arm about her shoulders. She began hastily to fumble in her handbag for her handkerchief. It dropped to the snowy ground. Astakhov bent over to pick it up, giving Lena time to hide her little nose and wet eyes in the high fur collar of her coat.

"Come, come, Lena, what's the use of all this?" said Astakhov in a loud facetious tone. But his wife still hid her face. "Cheer up, Lena, dear," he said, this time tenderly. "You know what the boys say— you can't fill your gas tank with tears, no matter how hot they are."

"All aboard." The express train moved out slowly and the outlines of the people on the platform grew increasingly fainter in the twilight. Lena Astakhova's fluttering handkerchief vanished from sight, and only the tall factory chimneys continued to wave to us with their long sleeves of smoke. Soon we picked up speed, and large and small stations flew past us so fast that we could not catch their names. On the first day of our trip we covered over seven hundred miles, stopping only to take water into our engine. As we swept past cities and villages, towers and signal stations—there were hundreds of them on our long stretch—the people cheered us and smiled at us, their eyes full of hope and gratitude. Young and old came running to meet our train at the smaller stations, which we passed at reduced speed. The people had no difficulty in guessing what freight our flat cars were carrying—a Mammoth can hardly be mistaken for a bicycle. Moreover, a poster covering the door of one of our cars depicted a KV with a proboscis instead of a gun, and paws instead of caterpillar treads. In the trunk of our animal was the mortally crushed figure of Hitler, and under its paws a pack of wolves with Nazi heads lay bleeding. "Our Soviet Mammoth will crush the Nazi Wolves" was the inscription on the poster, which a Red Army man named Teslya had drawn for us, and which met with roars of approval from everyone who saw it. "That's the way to do it! Kill the beasts!" was the general comment.

Farther and farther westward we rolled, over the land of our fathers, over the vast reaches of the Soviet Union. Boundless snow-covered farm fields merged with the sky at the horizon. Sometimes the train plunged into dense woods, and its roar, punctuated by the shrill cries of the engine, disturbed the tranquillity of century-old oaks and mighty firs covered with hoar-frost. The forest echoed this strident medley of sounds in softened tones, and in the clank and swish of the rushing train we felt the rhythm of our own motion. It seemed to us that the forest was not angry at us for violating its solemn peace, that on the contrary the very trees and bushes whispered: "Those were our own splendid boys who just roared past us." We felt that all these innumerable trees and bushes were greeting us and wishing us godspeed on our long journey, that every single one of them was one of us, a child of our native Soviet soil.

Rivers and rivulets, lakes and canals spread across our path, spanned by bridges of all lengths and sizes, pointing the way ahead. Our eyes delighted in numerous hydro-electric plants which utilized

31

the latent energy of our waters even in winter. We passed hundreds upon hundreds of factories and mills, railroad depots, machine and tractor stations and electric power stations. And we knew that all these rivers and canals and lakes and all those man-made buildings, from the gigantic plant where our tanks had been made to the small water pumps that fed our huge locomotive, were our own, our Soviet property. We felt that we were speeding westward to defend all these cities and factories and fields and farms and forests and rivers, to defend our own freedom as Soviet citizens against the savage hordes that had invaded us. We were proud of our assignment. We thought with grief and anger of that part of our land which had been temporarily overrun by the Nazis. That, too, we thought, is our own, our Soviet possession, and we must fight fiercely to recover it. Many among us came from the occupied territories. There was Georgi Konstantinov, the driver of the first tank, a Belorussian whose family had been left behind in his native Belorussia; there was Nikolai Pipa, the radio operator of the second machine, a son of the Ukraine. All of us desired as strongly as they did to hasten the day of deliverance for Belorussia and the Ukraine, for Odessa and

A huge tank is hoisted into place inside the factory, while the Russian crew stands ready to take over. *(Sovfoto from Artkino)*

Completed KV's and their crews lined up for the trip from factory to firing line. *(Sovfoto from Artkino)*

"The massive trees cracked under the caterpillars like pieces of sugar under the impact of a strong set of teeth." (Sovfoto)

"They had to climb the steep snow-covered bank of a ditch." (Sovfoto)

Novgorod. Every one on this train considered himself a loyal son of his great multi-national fatherland. We did not know exactly to what front we were going, but we knew that we were going to fight for our own Soviet Union.

The Tank Express rolled onward. The tankmen grew attached to the box cars with their little iron stoves and unpainted plank beds that still emanated the fragrant odor of fresh pine. Here, the tank crews did their various military duties, stood guard over the huge machines and spent their leisure time. They heated their tin plates on the stoves, and when the train stopped they went out to get water for their tea.

Mechanic Georgi Konstantinov had just returned from the flat car where he had spent several hours warming up his tank to protect it from a forty-five degree frost and a fierce wind.

"Well, how is it?" asked Tank Commander Yefimov.

"Fine, we won't let it freeze on us," replied the driver. Konstantinov was a swarthy broadshouldered energetic fellow with a serious expression. He knew the tanks better than anyone, and even technicians often consulted him on difficult problems. He had acquired his knowledge the hard way. Only twenty-three years old, he had already seen fighting on two fronts. He had taken part in the Khalkin Gol affair, and had seen the entire Finnish campaign on the Karelian Isthmus. Now he was on his way to fight his third war.

Another driver-mechanic, Eugene Dormidontov, a native of Moscow, was no less experienced. A husky, solidly built Russian with a gentle face and big shrewd gray eyes, he was the life of the company. He always managed to spread gaiety all around him, and even the phlegmatic and dreamy Vedishchev responded to his presence. He was also popular because of his ability to sing expressively. "Zhenia, sing us the *Eagle!*" "Zhenia, sing *Suleika*," were some of the requests showered upon him from every direction. The boys never tired of his performances. "Wait a minute," he would reply, "just let me get into the proper position." He would settle down comfortably on his berth near the window. He had picked this place because he liked to look at the passing landscape, and his musical repertoire always included songs that seemed to have been inspired by forests, fields or rivers.

The boys always listened to him in almost religious silence, crowding around him as he rendered some touching Georgian song about love and nightingales in his soft tender tenor. Vedishchev, the small radio operator with the girlish face and slow manner of speech, was particularly moved by such songs. In a friendly chat by the red-hot stove he once confided to me that what he loved above everything in the world was trees and gardens. All his life he had dreamed of becoming a gardener, of cultivating fruits and berries and producing a new species, like the famous botanist Michurin. He had been working on a state fruit farm and was deeply attached to his occupation. But the war had come and now he was a radio man.

"As soon as Hitler is smashed I'll go back to my job," he said with enthusiasm. "I want you all to come visit me there. You ought to taste the delicious apples I can grow." Vedishchev was the very best radio man in his outfit, according to his commander —ready to fight to the last to defeat the fascists.

Every morning and evening informal political talks were arranged for the crews. Astakhov himself presided over them. Removing his helmet and shoving back his auburn hair, he would announce: "And now I'll tell you what's happening in this wide world of ours." Radio kept the train in constant contact with outside events, and the tankmen were keenly interested in the progress of the war, especially on the Soviet-German front.

As we drew nearer the front, our men threw the car doors open more frequently. Dressed in padded coats and felt boots, they were oblivious to the cold and wind. "We've got to see whom we're overtaking and whom we're meeting, don't we?" they explained. During one stop, someone suddenly shouted: "Look, boys, there's a German tank! A trophy from the front!" Although most of our tankmen had seen action, and enemy tanks were no novelty to them, everybody ran up to the flat car on which a battered Nazi machine had been placed. "Get your class together, professor," shouted Dormidontov, inviting Konstantinov, who knew all about German tanks, to "give a lecture." In the twinkling of an eye, Konstantinov was lifted onto the car carrying the tank, from which he gave a three-minute talk describing the technical features and fighting qualities of the captured machine. "Now you can see for yourselves," he concluded, pointing to dozens of gaping holes in the German armor, "what a 'high' quality tank this is." He pronounced

Everywhere local residents with their families follow close behind advancing Red Army units to return to their liberated villages. *(Sovfoto)*

Residents of burned villages make temporary homes in dugouts. *(Sovfoto)*

A woman collective farmer returns home after the Germans' retreat to find her home in ruins. *(Sovfoto)*

Driven out of their homes by the Germans, several families take refuge in a single dugout. *(Sovfoto)*

the word 'high' with a sarcastic emphasis which drew gales of laughter from our men. "Our KV's surely have nothing to fear from this!"

"I wish we'd hurry up and get at them," observed Vedishchev, who was usually so quiet and patient.

The Tank Express was approaching the firing line. In a little over two days it had covered nearly 1,300 miles—a remarkable achievement in a country at war. All the credit for this goes to our railroad workers, and especially the highly experienced crew who had manned our engine during the last lap and who had been driving trains in the battle zone since the beginning of the war.

We began to hear the dull rumble of cannon in the distance. Our crews took their posts near their tanks, preparing to take them off the cars. As we heard the screech of halting brakes, we discerned a field-unloading platform in the semi-darkness of the night. A few minutes later our giant machines were safe on firm ground. We were at the front.

Chapter IV

SCIENCE AT THE FRONT

THE MAMMOTHS entered a silent snow-blanketed village, followed by two dozen armored machines of a lighter type, which gracefully manoeuvred between the houses and the hoar-covered willows.

Camouflaging the gigantic KV's was quite a problem. To station them in the village would have necessitated crushing gardens and fences and smashing outhouses. Yet the machines had to be concealed in a hurry, for morning was about to break and enemy aircraft might come over at any moment. Lieutenant Astakhov had his hands full. His tall silhouette was clearly visible against the snow as he bustled about the edge of the village.

"You can't call these machines; they're more like grain elevators. Just try to find a suitable place for them," he grumbled. Then he issued the following orders:

"Second Lieutenant Gomozov and Lieutenant Yefimov will occupy positions at the edge of the village, one to the right, the other to the left. Make believe you are houses."

On an incline which sloped down toward a small river near the village, Astakhov caught sight of an old bathhouse. The place was strategically situated for defending the village in case of an attack. "Of course you mustn't station yourself beside it," he said to Lieutenant Chilikin, "the enemy has surely taken note of it as a landmark. Get on top of it, you'll be the bathhouse itself."

Astakhov sent the two remaining machines to a small pine grove that looked black in the early blue twilight.

"I give you thirty minutes to camouflage yourselves so that nothing is noticeable," said the unit commander to the individual tank commanders.

When day came, enemy scouting planes crisscrossed the sky over the village, flying singly or in pairs, but they discovered nothing out of the ordinary. All the houses, real and sham, looked perfectly innocent with white smoke curling up from their chimneys. The two KV's at the edge of the village had been covered with white canvas simulating roofing, and stove chimneys had been set on the top, from which smoke was rising just as from the real chimneys on the houses beside them. To match the rest of the village, these new "houses" were surrounded with frosty trees, and they even had "outhouses" constructed of piles of discarded wood. The bathhouse by the river was also there, only slightly swollen. Instead of levelling it, our tank had smashed a wall and nosed inside, and the men had piled a layer of timber on top of it. As for the machines in the pine grove, they were well hidden by the trees.

After their long trip, our tankmen slept like logs for twelve hours, while sentinels kept a sharp watch in the village, and details kept the machines warm.

We were still at the freight depot when Senior Political Instructor Belanchevadze, Inspector of the Army Political Department, came up to us. He was full of snap and energy, with a shrewd mouth and thoughtful eyes. "I'm going to fight with you," he said.

Belanchevadze was a tank specialist and had been at the front since the beginning of hostilities. On the second day he made it his business to become acquainted with all the crews and had several talks with them. Then he paid a visit to headquarters and declared: "Many of your men have seen fighting before and that's a good thing. But you've had very little experience with the latest type of fighting, and that's bad."

Major Maximov, the commander of the battalion to which our five KV's were attached, was annoyed. He pointed out that all of us had seen action in this war. "That's not enough," insisted Belanchevadze. "Even if you had been here only two weeks ago you would be out of touch with the latest developments. Tank warfare is both an art and a science and, as you know, science is being constantly enriched by new data." To appease our major whose feelings had been somewhat hurt, the Political Instructor proceeded to illustrate his point by a few historical examples. He evoked the character of one of the greatest Soviet strategists, Frunze, who was always eager to increase his vast store of knowledge by studying the latest methods of fighting, never disdaining even seemingly unimportant details. "The last time you fought it was summer," he concluded. "Now it is winter. You fought in one type of machine; now you have another. And don't forget that

41

the enemy's tactics have undergone a radical change since June 1941."

The following day we understood the truth of the Political Instructor's warning when several truck loads of tankmen from a neighboring unit arrived from the front. We gave them a cordial reception in the biggest house in the village. The men of the two units soon became friends and exchanged experiences in lively conversations. Senior in rank among the guests was Major Segeda, a tank battalion commander. He was an expansive Ukrainian with sharp foxlike eyes. His face retained a jovial expression even when he was angry, and his recalcitrant forelock kept falling over his eyes and nose, concealing his frowns. The tanks of Segeda's unit had been manufactured at the same plant as ours, before its evacuation from Leningrad, and the men soon discovered that they had many mutual friends among the workers.

"Well, how are they getting along in the Urals?" Segeda asked.

"They live very well and work even better. They are resolved to crush the Nazis," replied Astakhov.

"They'll be able to supply the Leningrad front now, too," said Segeda. "Leningrad will get real

42

help now." The grim look on his face showed that he meant what he said.

Segeda's voice was emotional, high-pitched and somewhat raucous. He was evidently conscious of this defect, because he always tried to supplement his words by all sorts of other sounds or gestures, such as clicking his tongue or thumping on the table. When relating some battle incident, always involving tanks, of course, he would suddenly jump up from his seat, and imitate a tank turn with his corpulent figure; then he would bend down, take aim and "open fire" on his target by pounding the table or stamping with his boots. It was in this picturesque manner that he described one unusual tank attack in which he acted both as tank commander and driver-mechanic.

"That was a tough fight," he said. "The driver was wounded in the hand and I had to take his place. Our tank was charging an enemy strong point for the ninth time, after penetrating the main positions, accounting for over a hundred German troops, crushing a couple of guns and blowing up about a dozen pillboxes in a day of fighting. As we attacked, the frightened Fritzes and Hanses began to scatter, running all over the field. But there were among

43

them a few tank destroyers who were hiding in a trench with big bundles of hand grenades awaiting our approach.

"I dashed forward and knocked out the destroyers with my machine guns. Suddenly my gunner reported that we had no more shells left. 'Give it to them with the machine guns!' I shouted back. 'Comrade Major, our cartridges have given out, too!' he replied. 'All right,' I said. 'Just keep a good lookout from the top. We'll try to get them with our caterpillars.'

"I stepped on the gas as hard as I could and suddenly found myself close to the parapet of the biggest Nazi trench. 'There's a Fritz with a hand grenade!' I heard a voice from above. My tank crashed on. I looked through the slit, and right in front of me I saw a Nazi sticking his head out of the trench and reaching for his bundles of hand grenades. I stopped abruptly and automatically pressed the siren button. A shrill scream pierced the frozen air and frightened the German who ducked back into the trench. 'Imagine that!' I thought to myself. 'I might have known it would work well.' At that moment the German reappeared and again prepared to throw his grenades. 'Oo-oo-oo!' The stri-

Residents eagerly return to their villages once they are liberated from the enemy. *(Sovfoto)*

A Russian soldier returns to his home to find everything destroyed but the chimney. *(Sovfoto)*

Homeless Russians are forced to find shelter in German dugouts.
(Sovfoto)

Russian children whose parents were taken prisoner and home destroyed by the Germans. *(Sovfoto)*

dent call of the siren once again caused the Nazi to duck. 'Some fighter,' I thought. 'He hears a roar and thinks it's a shell. That kind of shell will last a long time.' The Nazi popped out again, and I was about to 'shoot' him with my horn, when suddenly a dull sound resounded from my cannon and a sheet of fire struck the Nazi straight in the face. He fell in a heap at the edge of the trench screaming like a pig and trying to cool his scorched snout by pressing it against the snow. It turned out that my gunner—his name is Kononov—had decided to supplement my siren artillery with a simple signal rocket and, training the gun on the German, had fired the rocket point blank. The Germans, apparently believing we had a secret weapon, were terrified by the howling noise and the multicolored flames.

"But after a while, the rockets, too, gave out—all we had left was the siren. The Germans must have guessed what was the matter for they came rushing out toward my machine shouting, 'Russ kaput! Russ kaput!' I opened the throttle wide and dashed full speed ahead trying to get them under my caterpillars. They jumped back into their trench and began to shower us with hand grenades. Then it flashed through my mind that we, too, had some 'lemons.'

45

'Open the lower hatch and prepare the grenades!' I yelled to Kononov, heading the tank toward the large trench where about two dozen Nazis were huddled together, still shouting *'Russ kaput.'* The tank lumbered ahead. I stopped it right athwart the trench with its bottom hatch open. Kononov did not have to be told what to do. He pelted the Nazis with our 'lemons' and in no time at all the whole group of 'tank wreckers' were silenced. The Nazis in the other trenches took to their heels.

"I glanced into the trench through the hatch and asked: 'Well, Fritz, who got the worst of the bargain?' There was no reply. 'You got what was coming to you, you so-and-sos!' I said as I left. 'Next time you won't shout *"kaput"* while we're around.'"

We learned that Major Segeda's unit had had much fighting experience and had scored a number of successes with the heavy KV tanks. During the last few weeks alone they had destroyed 93 German guns, 50 machine-gun nests, 10 trench mortars, 5 tanks and 20 redoubts; moreover, their caterpillars, tank artillery and machine guns had wiped out the equivalent of two German infantry regiments. First Class Sergeant Naidin, one of the gun commanders, smashed 11 German tanks although wounded several times. First Class Sergeant Tsekalov, a tank driver, had taken his KV into battle forty times. He had wiped out hundreds of Nazis and destroyed some 20 guns as well as several tanks and trucks. His tank had received many direct shell hits, and some fragments remained embedded in its armor. The machine did not suffer a single accident or break-down, thanks to the proficiency of its crew, and she was still going into battle like an old warhorse.

The modest accounts of the major and his men deeply impressed our own tankists filling them with the desire to emulate their comrades.

"And now let's get down to production problems," said Segeda. He wanted to acquaint the newly ar-rived tankmen with his experience in tank warfare under the difficult conditions prevailing on this front, and with the best methods of counteracting the various stratagems used by the enemy. Segeda's mechanics, radio operators and artillery men had long talks with the specialists of our KV unit. Our post was now seething with activity. Segeda's men did not limit themselves to oral instructions, they lent us a hand in installing various appliances in the tanks, drove them, showed us how to repair them or refuel them under enemy fire, and how and where to place infantry who were to be landed from tanks.

Two days later, our tankmen paid a visit to Segeda's unit and practiced on their machines under enemy fire. During all these exercises the men and commanders were in the highest spirits and full of gratitude to those who had organized the manoeuvres. Dormidontov said: "Our boys have learned many things they did not know before."

Following Belanchevadze's suggestion, the command decided on a partial exchange of tankmen. The less experienced of the newcomers were temporarily assigned to Segeda's unit for practical training; in exchange five veterans from his unit were assigned to Astakhov's. They were Corporal Bolshunov, who had 200 hours of tank driving in battle to his credit; First Class Sergeant Tenditny, who had led his tank into 28 attacks; Sergeant Gordeev, an expert at ramming; Sergeant Kononov, gun commander and Private Maschev, a gunner who had taken part in more than 20 battles. Our tankmen gave a rousing welcome to these men, two of whom had shown exceptional bravery in action. Gordeev had once driven a tank into a village, crushing two enemy guns. Discovering two more guns behind a stone wall, and having no room to turn, he had re-

Russian women weep for their dead. (*Sovfoto from Artkino*)

A mother without family or home. (*Sovfoto from Artkino*)

During a lull in the fighting Russian soldiers celebrate New Year's at the front. (Sovfoto)

A New Year's party is celebrated in the traditional way. (Sovfoto)

versed gears and crushed the other two guns by backing up, only to find himself showered with bullets from anti-tank rifles posted in a near-by attic. Gordeev had smashed right through the wall of the house, brought down the attic and exterminated the enemy riflemen with machine-gun fire. Kononov had distinguished himself by fighting for sixteen hours in a damaged machine surrounded by the enemy and holding his ground until he was rescued by Soviet reinforcements. The presence of such heroes in our midst gave us new heart for the coming battle.

One of the most interesting and instructive classes we had was devoted to studying the latest German regulations concerning the methods of fighting our heavy tanks. These regulations had been found on the body of a German anti-tank battery officer, or, as Major Segeda put it, were "crushed out" of him when he and all his men were surprised by one of our tanks. The document was called: *How to Fight Russian Heavy Tanks,* and the first paragraph ran as follows: "The fact that the enemy employs heavy tanks which cannot be crushed by German tanks presents us with a problem which must be solved." We were glad to hear that the Germans were anxiously seeking a solution to this problem, and were somewhat impatient to know the results of their intellectual efforts in this direction. The text that followed was rather disappointing: aside from furious vituperations which only stressed the Nazis' impotence in dealing with our KV's, it contained a mere rehash of well-known methods of anti-tank warfare. "The German tanks," the regulations read on, "are designed to destroy enemy tanks in offensive operations under normal conditions. But the equipment developed heretofore has proved inadequate for accomplishing this task in the present war. Thus it becomes the task of shock infantry detachments to deal with the super-tanks." We listened with the greatest interest to the instructions issued to these "shock infantry detachments" so we could prepare ourselves to give them a fitting reception. The last of these instructions aroused great hilarity among our men. "Every soldier," the German booklet promised, "who destroys a Russian tank weighing 26, 32 or 52 tons will be cited for an award. In addition, every soldier who has a 26 or 32-ton tank to his credit, will be granted one week's furlough with permission to go home. For the destruction of a 52-ton tank a two-weeks' furlough will be granted."

"So our Mammoths are worth a two-weeks' leave of absence," smilingly observed Astakhov.

"Nothing of the sort," shouted Dormidontov angrily. "Just let me have one fight with them and I'll give every one of those swine a furlough that will never expire!"

Chapter V

NEW YEAR'S EVE

THAT MORNING Eugene Dormidontov was one of the first to go out to his machine which he had left in the pine grove the preceding night. He walked quickly across the vegetable gardens to the group of pines, looking carefully for the hiding place of his tank. His well trained eye soon distinguished it from the other tank by the particular way in which the camouflage twigs had been arranged. He briskly removed the tarpaulin cloth that covered the hatch, and smiled with satisfaction as he read the inscription that had been put on the turret when the tank was still in the factory: "Happy New Year!"

"So you wish me a Happy New Year, little Mammoth, do you?" said the driver gently to his steel-clad machine. "That's right. Today is December thirty-first. Many happy returns of the day to you!"

Having thus exchanged New Year greetings with

his tank, Dormidontov climbed into it for his routine inspection. His holiday mood caused him to do his job even more meticulously than usual. Other members of his crew, Shishov, Solovyov and Pisarev, soon joined him.

"Hello, boys," said Eugene. "We may have a chance to extend our New Year's greeting to the Germans tonight, so take a good look at everything."

The boys had begun following his advice even before he gave it. Solovyov, the assistant mechanic, was at work in the motor compartment with some old rags, and Pisarev, the gunner, lovingly dusted the copper cases and dove-colored steel heads of the anti-tank shells.

"These will be nice presents for the Heinies," he said to Dormidontov. "I'm sure they can hardly wait to get them." Then he tested the lock and started the turret motor to see whether his gun could easily be turned "in all sixteen directions," as he used to say. The turret had barely made one turn, when from outside came the angry voice of Kalinichev, the tank commander.

"What the devil are you doing?" he shouted. "Are you blind or what? You're busting up the whole woods with your gun!"

53

"But I'm not shooting," Pisarev mumbled as he climbed out through the upper hatch. He understood Kalinichev's anger when he saw that the long barrel of his gun had scattered a dozen fine pine trees that had been planted during the night to camouflage the machine.

The whole crew at once proceeded to put the overthrown trees back into their original positions. But the tank commander continued to grumble: "You knocked off all the hoar-frost. We can't have camouflage without it. I ought to make you breathe on every one of those pines to make them look frosty."

This little incident did not disturb Dormidontov's good spirits. As was his custom, he sang one merry song after another.

Evening came with the sky as blue and the air as crisp and frosty as in the morning. The temperature dropped to thirty below zero. The tankmen assembled in a spacious hut to get dinner in their little pots. They sat on fragrant rye straw which had been spread on the floor, and kept their eyes fixed on their commander, Astakhov, and on Battalion Commissar Kharchenko. The two officers sat in the corner under two icons, evidently preparing to address their men.

When Astakhov rose, all talking ceased at once, and the straw stopped rustling.

"Comrades, we may have to fight tonight," he declared. "And then again we may not have to. The Germans facing us seem to be nervous about something. In other words, better forget about going to sleep. Everyone must be on the alert, and at his post in his machine."

Commissar Kharchenko spoke as always with emotion, and his appeal went straight to our hearts. "As you see we are going to celebrate the New Year of 1942 in our fighting machines. The Nazi swine had expected to have us locked up in their concentration camps, behind barbed wire, by this time. Instead, we are going to give them the beating of their lives. Think, comrades, of this symbolic fact: our unit has arrived at the front at the birth of 1942. Our whole country has passed to the counter-offensive, and Hitler's gangsters are being pushed back along the entire front. This new year, 1942, will see the turning of the tide. It begins tonight. At exactly twelve we shall celebrate the event by drinking a glass of vodka. But if the order to attack comes at that hour, forget your glasses, and load your guns. We will celebrate New Year's Eve by preparing coffins for the Germans."

Our men greeted the conclusion of the Commissar's speech with cheers and laughter, then plunged their spoons into a steaming pea soup full of meat, followed by a heaping plate of *kasha*.

"Fill up for the New Year!" cried Nesterenko, the cook, in merry tones, as he ladled the portions out of thermos containers.

Only a few hours remained before midnight. Our men removed the tarpaulin and the camouflage pines from the tanks. The gun turrets were stripped for action and everything was in readiness for commencing the New Year's battle. The Germans were still nervous. From time to time we could hear the bark of their long-range guns, hurling random shells across No Man's Land. A machine gun rattled spasmodically, then stopped.

"Those scoundrels over there are shivering in their boots, both in the literal and figurative meaning of the word," said Pisarev. "I can tell it by the way they're firing."

Our artillery refrained from replying to the desultory German fire, in order not to reveal our positions. It was a duel of nerves. It would have been easy for our gunners to silence an enemy battery, but we were preparing for much more serious business—a sudden onslaught that would defeat the enemy on an entire sector of the front.

About half an hour before midnight, a sudden command rang out in vibrant tones: "At ease! Celebrate the New Year, each crew for itself!" Apparently the Germans were not preparing anything serious for that night, nor were we ready to take the offensive.

I was in Astakhov's tank. The machine immediately resounded with joyful commotion. Tenditny, the driver, drew from his bag a pint of vodka, in a blue bottle that looked like a steel shell. There was just enough in it for five men; the liquor had been issued by the mess sergeant and it was the real thing.

"Get your cups ready," said Tenditny. Everybody eagerly held out his enameled iron drinking pot. The "fuel"—as vodka is called hereabouts—was soon dispensed. Refreshments were sizzling on the electric stove—canned meat deliciously flavored with laurel leaves and tomatoes.

"To the health of our supreme Commander-in-Chief, Stalin," Astakhov said solemnly in the deepest bass he could muster.

"To the health of the workers who gave us our tanks!" added Predannikov.

57

"To victory in 1942!" exclaimed the men in chorus. They clinked their cups and drained them simultaneously as befits a well-trained crew.

The air was filled with the voices of men. The tank sounded like a hen-house. One question was on everyone's lips and in everyone's mind: "When do we start fighting?" Suddenly the lid of our tank opened and our festive company caught a glimpse of a patch of starry sky, which was at once blotted out by Dormidontov's grinning face. "May I invite you to the New Year tree at our tank?" he said engagingly. His face vanished again.

The idea of a tree, and particularly of a tree at Dormidontov's, aroused general enthusiasm. Everybody tried to get out of the tanks, and soon a crowd of guests from the whole battalion gathered around Dormidontov's tank which was stationed at some distance, near the most graceful of all the pines. As our group came closer, we were dumbfounded at the spectacle before us. A pine tree that had been growing on this spot since the day it was planted was handsomely decorated with hundreds of what seemed to be toys. Though it was not lighted up by candles, it glimmered with a gold and silvery sheen from the soft moonlight which played on the

58

surface of the toys. Golden beams dancing on the copper of cartridges and shells assumed a silvery tone when reflected by empty tin cans. In addition, the tree bore many other clever decorations, such as cigarette boxes, biscuits, yellow bast ribbons, colored pieces of paper, newspaper pages and even parachute straps taken from the wrecked German plane that lay on the field near our camp. Dormidontov's inventive genius was responsible for this improvised masterpiece. We later learned that this expansive fellow, refusing to accept the idea of a New Year's Eve without some sort of celebration, had conspired with his crew to arrange this surprise party. But what pleased the guests more than anything else was not the tree, but the KV tank standing close to it, with the inscription, "A Happy New Year!" gaily lettered on its turret. Dormidontov himself, the arch-contriver of the party, was, however, absent, and the role of host was played by his tank commander, Kalinichev, while Kharchenko, the battalion commissar, walked about with a satisfied air exchanging jokes with the men and challenging them to show him another such tree in the whole battalion.

The mystery of Dormidontov's absence was

cleared up a few minutes later, when Kalinichev declared: "On behalf of our crew, I invite you to listen to Father Frost, who is visiting our battalion and will take part in our celebration. Father Frost (the Russian Santa Claus) has the floor." At that very moment, to the delight of our tankmen, the massive figure of snow-covered Father Frost stepped forth from behind the decorated pine tree. He wore a fur coat turned inside out and a long beard reaching to the ground. This traditional attire was appropriately supplemented by an automatic in his hand, a number of hand grenades slung around his belt and a tankman's helmet on his head.

"Happy New Year, friends," began Father Frost in a stage bass.

"It's Eugene! We might have known it!" exclaimed Dormidontov's admirers.

"Well, Father Frost, let's hear something good!"

"Watch out for your nose, Father Frost, it might freeze off!"

Everyone was in high spirits.

"I have come to join you at the front," Father Frost went on, this time speaking in a serious tone, "to fight in the just cause of the Russian people, shoulder to shoulder with you, to help you to annihilate

60

the accursed Nazis." Then he broke out into song:

Who whistles and howls in the pine trees?
Is it the wind or the rushing rivers?
No, it is I, Father Frost, on a visit
To my wintry domains.

Today I have seen how the blizzards
Have blanketed the forests in snow,
Today I have looked through a peep-hole
Into an enemy blockhouse.

I paid a call on the Fritzes and Heinies
And got an idea of their plight
What are the odds for the Nazis
To emerge the winners from this war?

"And, comrades, I can assure you," Father Frost resumed in prose, "that their chances are rather slim. Their teeth are chattering with cold, and hunger drives them to sing doleful songs. I walked freely among the Germans and they were too scared to ask for my pass. I tweaked their sentries by their noses and they found themselves a frozen white chunk instead of a nose. To become better acquainted with them I firmly shook their hands and even their feet. But no sooner did I grab one of their thin leather shoes than I found myself holding a stiff piece of wood instead of a foot. And the result was always that a Nazi soldier had to be taken to a hospital where wood replaced his foot for good.

"At one place, old fool that I am, I was attracted by the charms of a passing female who walked along the streets, elegantly dressed, with cloak, hat and neat little boots—a most bewitching lady she was. I followed her. I'll remember my youth, I thought to myself, and try somehow to make a hit. At last I caught up with her and gently pinched her silk-stockinged legs. The dainty creature kicked up her heels as though in greeting and moved on with mincing little steps.

" 'I guess I can proceed to storm the fort,' I thought, and decided to outflank her with a kiss on the cheek. I wheeled round on one caterpillar, stepped on the gas, and pounced on my enchant-ress. But, horror! My beard came into contact with the stinking prickly moustache of a German corporal. I drew back in loathing and pulled out his moustache together with the skin under it. I'm still spitting to rid my mouth of the after-taste of that foul contact.

But while I will finally get rid of it, the German corporal will never forget the gentle kiss he received from Father Frost.

"So make use of my services, tankmen, to beat the Nazis to a pulp. I am a loyal friend of yours, your best ally. You are a splendid lot. It will be a cinch for you to lick that loathsome gang of Heinies. They have not a chance against you.

"But I must warn you to treat me with care. If you forget to empty your radiators, I will freeze them and your machines won't move. If you don't keep your weapons well greased, the parts will stick together, and your guns and rifles won't fire. Let us be good partners and form a strong alliance in order to insure our victory over Hitler's frost-bitten gangsters. For my part, I undertake to freeze the Nazis every step, to turn their bestial drunken brains to ice, so that you will be able to apply to me the words of our great poet Nekrassov, slightly paraphrased with your permission:

> He walks among trees and his step
> Cracks the frozen surface of the water
> And on his patriarchal beard
> Plays the sun of glorious victory."

Hearty applause from fur-clad hands was Father Frost's reward. The tankmen were elated over this New Year's speech and were enthusiastic about Dormidontov who had acted his part perfectly.

* * *

That night I also visited the tank commanded by Second Lieutenant Dayev. His men—later nicknamed the "bachelor's crew"—also celebrated the New Year by drinking wine and keeping their machine open, but ready for action. Against the white background of the tank's turret I could read an inscription in letters of scarlet: "Avenge Our Beloved Soviet Girls." There is a story behind this inscription. Earlier in the day, I had noticed a black-haired young tankman in neat fur-lined overalls busy painting the words, "Let us avenge our Soviet girls," on the turret of his tank which was stationed near Dormidontov's. Three times the tankman stepped back a few yards, carefully examined his handiwork, and returned to touch up one letter or another that apparently did not satisfy him. Finally he stood at some distance from the turret absorbed in thought. Then he walked firmly toward the tank and dipping the splinter of wood he had been using as a brush

Tankmen checking their arms before an attack. *(Sovfoto)*

Tanks deploying for action as shells burst around them. *(Sovfoto)*

New tanks heading towards advanced lines. *(Sovfoto)*

Russian tankists in ambush receiving final battle instructions. *(Sovfoto)*

into the paint pot, he added, with a flourish, the word
"beloved." As he stood obviously pleased with his
masterpiece, Second Lieutenant Dayev, the tank
commander, came up, read the inscription and began
to argue with him. I could hear the following exchange of words between the two men:

"Did I tell you to put in that extra word?"

"No, you didn't."

"Then why did you do it?"

"It's a nice word, Comrade Commander, and
there was a little space left."

"I know it's a nice word," said the commander
angrily, "only it didn't come out very well. Now
you've got a veritable column of words. Why not
write a whole declaration of love while you're at
it?" he added ironically.

The tankman stood with downcast eyes. It was
hard for him to admit that he had made a mistake.
And the commander simply could not calm himself.
He mumbled the inscription to himself several
times, sarcastically stressing the word "beloved."

Suddenly the tankman stepped forward and said:

"Why, the word is very appropriate indeed, Comrade Commander. The memory of Zlotsva came
back to me." The lieutenant's features underwent

65

a sharp change. His face was suddenly gloomy and stern. Without a word he cast a hasty glance at the turret with the scarlet inscription. His lips trembled and one could see in his grief-stricken eyes that he was trying to utter that one word "beloved." Then he made a sharp turn to the right and walked away.

As I approached Dayev's tank I recalled this scene and asked the crew: "Boys, tell me, what girls are you going to avenge? Where have you left them?"

"We shall avenge them all," said Dayev evasively. He was obviously embarrassed.

"But still . . . could you not mention some names?"

"Lida was left behind, wasn't she?" said the young tankman who had painted the inscription.

The ice was finally breaking.

"Yes, she has remained at Zlotsva," said Dayev softly, looking dreamily into space.

I had not the heart to insist. But Dayev went on of his own accord:

"If I had not been wounded I would have taken her along with me. She even came to see me in the hospital and brought me flowers and handkerchiefs. Then they suddenly transferred me elsewhere."

"We'll find our girls yet and deliver them from the Nazis. You see, the same thing happened to all four of us," another member of the crew said resolutely.

Each of the men confided his story to me and told me the name of the girl he had left behind in occupied territory. When they raised their cups filled with wine to welcome the New Year, they uttered a passionate vow to rescue and avenge their sweethearts.

* * *

That night no alarm was sounded and no encounter with the enemy took place. But the crews received the following field order: all the commanders of the tank battalion were to put on white gowns and skis, take hand grenades and automatics and go out to reconnoiter during the night.

Chapter VI

THE MARCH OVER THE ICE

THE COMMANDER of the unit to which our tank battalion belonged explained to us the importance of Lake Ilmen. Five rivers flow into it from the south. Ranging in width from seventy-five meters to half a kilometer, these rivers absorb dozens of tributaries. The lake itself and the river mouths afford the best natural protection for troops on the defensive, and ever since autumn the Germans had been holding this excellent line. It had been their main support for the blockade of Leningrad. During the winter, they had strengthened it by erecting a large number of fortifications: strong points, trenches and barbed-wire entanglements. They had laid mine fields, and set up batteries of trench mortars and heavy guns. The entire area for hundreds of kilometers south of the lake was converted into a powerfully fortified district.

68

Taking the oath prior to an engagement. *(Sovfoto)*

A tank-borne infantry detachment rolls into battle. *(Sovfoto)*

Infantry attacking under cover of tanks. *(Sovfoto)*

Infantry supported by tanks storm the enemy's fortifications. *(Sovfoto)*

"That is why I have asked you to part for one day from your beloved caterpillars, comrade tankmen, and to take to your skis for a deep reconnaissance operation," the commander concluded.

Within twenty-four hours our tankmen on skis, under the command of Major Maximov, covered about forty kilometers. Dressed in white hoods, the scouts penetrated far into the frosty forest and onto the lake itself. With infinite caution so as not to be heard by the Germans, they bored holes in the ice to gauge its thickness.

After a day's rest, the tank battalion received the field orders for which they had been so impatiently waiting. They were instructed to cross Lake Ilmen and its tributaries during the night, penetrate thirty to forty kilometers behind the enemy's lines and launch a surprise attack on the flank of his main forces in the Staraya Russa area. Their objective was to encircle the 290th Infantry Division and the Skull-and-Bones SS Division of the 16th Army. As dusk fell, the engines began to hum and our battalion set out from its temporary camp.

Our five KV's started off with a thunderous roar that shook the earth. One could hear the rattle of the window panes in the peasant houses and the

69

dull thud of the tree trunks felled by our machines as they plunged through the woods. A raging blizzard conveniently covered our approach to the starting point of our offensive. On the outskirts of a small village we halted for the last time before the decisive thrust, to have our tanks inspected. We had to reach the battle area in perfect order—a difficult operation under the circumstances, for several water barriers separated us from our objective.

Lieutenant Astakhov made the rounds of the tanks accompanied by the chief engineer. "How's your machine?" "In perfect order," replied the tankmen in one voice.

Tarpaulins were removed from the guns and machine guns, shells were prepared and cartridge disks mounted. We had to be ready for any emergency. It was not impossible that the enemy might discover our presence sooner than we wished, and that fighting would start at once.

The tank column was accompanied by an infantry group which was to form a landing party. The machines at the head carried sappers whose assignment was to destroy the anti-tank mines. The infantrymen were ordered to take their places on the tanks. The storm was so furious that the order was scarcely audible as it passed along from tank to tank.

The white bodies of the tanks suddenly seemed to swell as white-cloaked infantrymen holding white automatics in their hands clambered on the machines. Despite the darkness, the monstrous silhouettes of the KV's were sharply distinguishable in the long column of several dozen tanks, which advanced with a thunderous clanking.

A dash of about ten kilometers and Lake Ilmen was before us. Its waters are not very deep, but they always teem with fish, especially since the war, for all fishing has stopped, even at the height of the season. In winter, the volume of water in the lake is greatly reduced; the severe frosts freeze it almost to its floor.

The heavy tank on which I was riding together with a group of infantrymen cautiously lumbered forward across the ice. We were ordered to jump off and walk alongside. Old Ilmen, as though annoyed by the sudden disturbance of its nocturnal peace, creaked and groaned as if shaken by a storm. The fifty-ton machines—this meant a pressure of 300 pounds per square centimeter of ice—caused the ice to crack with a strange tinkling sound, and on places

71

where the ice did not reach the bottom, its surface could be seen palpably bending under their weight. The other heavy machines were not permitted to move along the tracks of the first ones, but branched off to the right or left. Finally the lake was left behind.

We now had to cross the river near the Nazi lines. Because of the current, the ice on the river was much thinner, and had to be reinforced in order to support the weight of the heavy tanks. A few minutes before we came up, tankmen from another unit who had failed to take the necessary precautions met with a serious accident. In the middle of the river which was only a hundred meters wide, one of the heavy tanks crashed through the ice. The crew barely managed to save itself through the upper hatch.

Our engineers had prepared two thousand logs which they were supposed to spread over the ice and let freeze in. But we had arrived ahead of schedule, the Ilmen was already behind us, and the log-laying was still in progress. What was to be done? We could not afford to lose a minute. It was midnight. In a few hours day would break and the enemy air force would discover us before the completion of our first crossing. It was imperative to negotiate a fast crossing of the river which formed the outer wall of the fascist defense area. Once this wall was passed, we could "promenade" along, fighting our way to any part of the German fortifications we chose.

Although no logs were as yet in sight, holes had already been cut in the ice so that water could be taken from the lake to pour over the logs, thus giving them a new coat of ice. Our tankmen snorted at the sight of these holes: what good were they without the logs? Someone asked sarcastically if they were intended for some foolish wolf to stick his tail into so that he might catch fish, as the fox advised in Krylov's well-known fable. I confess that I was not alone in wishing that the chief of our engineers' detachment might soon find himself in the unenviable position of that wolf.

Every passing minute threatened our carefully planned operation with failure. But, once again, necessity proved the mother of invention. "Let's demolish the nearest village and use the timber from its houses to bridge the ice," suggested Major Max-

73

imov to our sappers. "But how will you get them here?" they asked. "We'll use our tanks, and then at least our advance can proceed."

No sooner said than done. An hour and a half later, our tanks brought a whole trainload of beams from the nearest village. Overjoyed at this unexpected solution to their problem, our sappers enthusiastically fell to work. We were sorry to have to tear down the houses of the collective farmers, but we had no other choice. They were the only means at hand to pave our way to victory. By tearing down the houses of one village we would be able to recapture scores and hundreds of others from the Nazis. We looked on as the water drawn up by pumps froze and cemented the bridge of logs with ice. On some of the logs we noticed odds and ends such as a housewife's threaded needle which had apparently been stuck into a wall and forgotten there, or bits of flowered paper or newspaper.

Soon the small and medium tanks crossed the river one after another, followed by the cautiously crawling heavy KV's. We were now on the opposite bank, and the Germans had not yet noticed us. Four powerful machines took the tank that had been submerged in tow. At a given signal, thousands of units of horsepower yanked the fifty-ton machine out of the water throwing up heaps of ice as they dragged it to the shore. The river looked as though it had been split in two by a gigantic battering ram. The machine itself was an unusual sight; covered with stalagmites and stalactites, with a trunk of ice instead of a gun, it looked like some monster of the ice age horrible enough to frighten any but the stoutest warriors. It took two hours of hard work to unfreeze it. At last its motor started and all the other apparatus began to function. Its crew, on the brink of death only a few hours ago, was in the highest spirits. "She is proof against fire and water," they joked gaily as they bustled about their machine.

Our column resumed its advance through woods and swamps. Day began to break when, still unnoticed by the enemy, we approached a second crossing. The sappers worked with gusto, carrying logs on their shoulders for several kilometers for the crossing, and soon a second bridge was laid for our tanks. It was broad daylight now. The German soldiers could hardly believe their eyes when they saw a whole column of tanks moving along the valleys which constituted their line of defense. They were taken completely by surprise. The Nazi artillery had

75

relied on infantry patrols, but that night the patrols failed to sound the alarm, having been quietly wiped out by our ski detachments.

Having crossed the river we outflanked the Nazis. Their confusion was indescribable; they had not imagined that our tanks could cross the frozen surface of Lake Ilmen and two rivers besides. The German guns had to make a ninety-degree turn to the left before opening fire. The first enemy shells burst on our bridge. "Shut the hatches! Watch the enemy!" Astakhov commanded. The infantry took cover behind the advancing machines. Although their ranges had been taken long ago, the Nazis were apparently too frightened to fire accurately. Our sappers who at first had scattered along both sides of the bridge, now ran back to it and resumed their work, helping to get the rest of the tanks to the opposite bank.

Astakhov had already crossed the river. Enemy shells and mines were coming dangerously close to our bridge. A few sappers were wounded, but none left his post. They bravely hammered back into place those logs that had been jerked out by the crossing tanks. But the German fire gradually grew more accurate. The crossing seemed doomed; a few

Red Army men of a tank-borne detachment taking German soldiers prisoner. *(Sovfoto)*

Tankmen of a Guards unit escorting German war prisoners. *(Sovfoto)*

War-weary women and children beside the ruins of their home. *(Sovfoto)*

Young brothers being treated for wounds inflicted by the Germans. *(Sovfoto)*

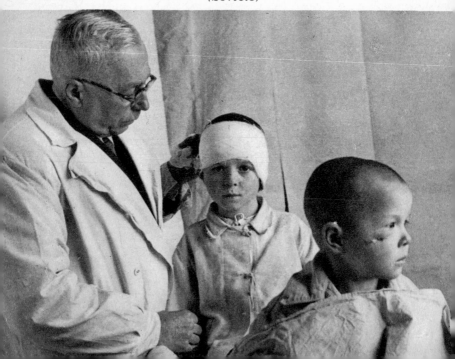

more seconds, and two big shells tore up the logs, causing two enormous geysers of water mixed with ice. The whole bridge began to heave. Suddenly a new explosion came with a roar: but this time it was Astakhov's tank which had fired. Having located an enemy battery, he at once began to pound it. Two or three other tanks opened fire and the German battery was silenced.

During this engagement, none of our men was killed, but two sappers fell into a hole in the ice. They swam frantically in their efforts to keep afloat and were finally pulled out by their comrades. While our sappers rushed to repair the damaged bridge and to build another one a short distance from the first, I ran to their wounded comrades who had been placed near one of the tanks. The forty-degree frost froze their drenched hoods into rigid armor. They looked like two white coffins made of ice in which two human faces could be discerned. An army surgeon and his orderlies used sappers' shovels to hack off the wounded men's frozen clothes. From the boys' drawn cheekbones and clenched jaws it could be seen that they were suffering terribly, but it was absolutely necessary to remove the ice in which they were encased in order to stop any further bleeding.

Blood was still flowing from their injured legs and arms with such force that it seeped through their clothes and thawed up the ice around them, dyeing it a deep red with a tinge of gold. By the time the two boys had their wounds dressed and were carried to an ambulance, the last tank of our column had crossed the river and was lumbering along the opposite bank. Battalion Commissar Kharchenko jotted down their names: Malushin and Yeremin. "Never mind, boys," he told them as they drove off, "you'll get well and there'll be another chance for you to show the stuff you're made of. Thanks for getting us across. In settling accounts with the enemy we won't forget what they did to you."

Apparently Astakhov's fire had effectively silenced the enemy batteries, for half an hour later we had reached a third water barrier without German interference. The familiar front-line din of rifles and machine guns once again struck our ears. It was caused by our advanced infantry detachments which were now engaging the enemy flank and rear. We proceeded to organize our third crossing. The operation proved easy this time, and was notable for the exemplary application of a classic military stratagem. When we reached the appointed place, a Nazi bomber appeared in the sky. We were ordered to take cover under the snowdrifts in the forests where we lay still while the enemy plane busily bombed a dummy bridge of branches and brushwood which our sappers had thoughtfully created.

When the Nazi flyer, obviously satisfied with his achievement, flew back to his base, our battalion quickly dashed across the river over a bridge which had been concealed under a coat of snow. Then we advanced across seven to eight kilometers of swampy grounds—not without experiencing some difficulties, for even during the winter a bog may prove as miry for a tank as during the summer. One of our medium machines sank in the mire to its very turrets piling up masses of hot peat as it struggled to disengage itself. After the machine was rescued, our command began to look for a different path. Sparse woods extended along one side of the bogs. "Trample down the woods and clear the way for the column!—in my opinion, a job for your KV tanks," said Major Maximov turning to Astakhov. "What do you say?"

A quick inspection of the woods revealed that

most of the trees were aspens, willows and young pines measuring perhaps fifteen centimeters in diameter—no obstacle to our Mammoths. Led by Astakhov, the column of heavy tanks cut down the trees as though they were a light picket fence. Soon the road was cleared, and our advancing tanks reached a new water barrier, about 300 meters wide, with steep banks rising as high as twenty meters. This time the Germans were not taken by surprise. On the opposite bank they fiercely resisted the assault of our advance infantry detachments, amidst deafening fire from mortars and automatics. But the Nazis were yet to learn what it meant to have in their rear, almost under their noses, the long-barreled guns of our powerful land fortresses.

Major Maximov ordered his battalion to deploy for charging the enemy and to open fire upon his positions across the river. "Lieutenant Astakhov!" he said. "You remain on this shore and take command. Direct your fire so as to cover my movement." The Major himself, with small tanks in dispersed formation, dashed across the ice.

The sudden appearance of Soviet armor which seemed to have emerged from the frozen river stunned the enemy. From the leading tanks the con-

80

Children shot by the Hitlerites. (Sovfoto)

A baby searches the face of its mother killed by the Germans. (Sovfoto from Artkino)

Camouflaged sleigh-borne troops prepare to advance in the wake of a tank. *(Sovfoto from Artkino)*

Red Army men advancing toward the enemy under cover of a tank. *(Sovfoto)*

fusion in the German camp could be seen clearly. Soon the enemy fire became desultory. Maximov with the units commanded by Fetlikhin and Maslov smashed at the first line of Nazi blockhouses, while Astakhov maintained a withering fire to cover the advancing Russian tanks. Simultaneously, the sappers began to put up a new wooden flooring to permit the passage of the heavy machines. Twilight fell. Under enemy fire, but without losing any men or machines, we crossed the fourth river.

We had now been in action for twenty-four hours. No one had eaten anything or even thought of eating. We thought only of establishing ourselves firmly in our newly won positions. The Germans retreated, abandoning their blockhouses, guns and dead. Our group commander ordered a small respite or, more accurately, a short period of preparation for a fierce new battle. The tankmen climbed out of their machines adjusting their sweaters and overalls. They were unrecognizable, their faces smeared with oil and blackened with soot. Although weary from the day-long battle, they refused to rest, proceeding instead to fill up their empty munitions cases and fuel tanks. One tank driver who was about to doze off drew a few angry words from Dormidontov who scolded him for "indulging in illusions that this was the time for sleep." But somehow we managed to get a two-hour rest. The tankmen fully deserved it. Their advance across the frozen rivers in heavy tanks was a great and unprecedented achievement. Our men felt that they had accomplished something significant although they knew that the big battles were still ahead.

Chapter VII

FIRST BATTLES, FIRST TROPHIES

FIVE KILOMETERS ahead of us was the village of Yuryevo, the terminus of the railroad, now transformed into a Nazi strong point. Our plans called for its capture at any cost.

Water barriers were again the principal obstacle to our advance. A river 450 meters wide—the fifth on our path—separated us from Yuryevo. At daybreak, our battalion deployed for battle, while the tanks waited under cover of the oak woods along the bank. Our assignment was to support the formations on our left. We reconnoitered in the dawn. The blizzard that had blinded us the day before had subsided; a clear moon was shining and the cold had become more intense. Thick layers of hoar gathered on the trees near the tanks, for the machines exhaled warm air as their mighty mechanisms breathed and labored.

Leaving our tanks, we moved silently in the early morning mist to the very edge of the river we had to cross. Through our binoculars we could discern the hazy outlines of logs and beams disposed along the opposite bank and apparently intended to look like the remains of last year's floating operations. We assumed that these fortifications were partly real and partly sham. Two recently built water towers were used by the enemy as observation posts. A barely perceptible stream of air rising from the deep gullies on the other side betrayed the breathing of the Nazis in the dugouts and timbered earthworks.

I looked at Major Maximov's swarthy, oblong face. He had put down his binoculars and was looking around in a rather nonchalant manner. Suddenly his gray eyes gleamed, and he said in a resolute voice: "Let's go."

We returned to our positions near the woods. The Major announced his plan of attack: "We'll ask our artillery to give them a matinee performance, blast all those rat holes and knock down the observation towers. Then we'll dash across with our light and medium tanks without laying pontoons. It worked last night, didn't it?" A brave and resolute commander, Major Maximov intended to lead the attack

84

in one of the vanguard tanks. The heavy machines were to cross later under the command of Commissar Kharchenko.

In accordance with our plan, our artillery opened a heavy barrage on the opposite bank. Protected by this fire, our tanks with infantrymen placed on them dashed across. The Germans had scattered anti-tank mines on the frozen surface of the water—we called them "pancakes" because of their shape. Apparently they had not seriously believed that we would try to cross in winter, otherwise they would have covered the mines with ice. Our sappers jumped down and removed the green disks of these explosives with great dispatch. "Better not eat those pancakes," Major Maximov warned them jovially.

The Germans directed a heavy fire from guns and mortars on the frozen river. But their shells failed to pierce the thick layer of ice and the tanks continued their advance. Then the Germans played their last card. They sent out five Junker planes to prevent us from crossing. One after another heavy bombs dropped on the ice causing ear-splitting explosions and shaking the entire shore. But the tanks sped on skilfully manoeuvring around the bomb-craters, and reached the opposite bank. During this operation only one of our medium tanks failed to cross. A stream of water caused by an exploding bomb temporarily blinded its driver who plunged into the icy bomb-hole. But only the rear end of the tank was submerged, and its crew escaped unharmed.

On the opposite bank a pitched battle developed between our tanks and the enemy anti-tank defenses. We now faced the Germans' last and most important link in their chain of fortifications on this sector of the front. The entire two-kilometer stretch between the river and the village was an intricate web of mines, barbed-wire entanglements and pill-boxes which spat fire and death on our advancing group, while the railroad station and the village poured out a heavy artillery barrage against our positions in the rear. But our tanks and infantry pressed on, outflanking the Nazis on both sides. Some of our smaller vanguard tanks struck mines or were hit by shells. Seeing them stop or spin helplessly around I regretted that our Mammoths were still on the other bank—those giant fortresses would have been impervious to the "pancake" mines or anti-tank guns. But the river and the enemy air force prevented them from joining in the assault. They helped us, however, from a distance, their power-

86

ful guns smashing the German entrenchments and strewing the ground with the corpses of Nazi rifle-men.

At 6 P.M. Major Maximov, supported by the fire of his whole battalion, rushed the village. Our infantrymen and sappers mounted on tanks wiped out the Nazi garrison with bayonets and hand grenades. The day was ours. Now the heavy tanks moved up across the newly erected pontoons.

The local inhabitants who had been hiding in cellars, behind snow drifts and in the woods emerged to greet us. "So our boys have returned after all," they said, weeping with joy. There were no men among them—only women and children, ragged, emaciated, grimy from their long stay in improvised hiding places under the ground.

Most of the houses had remained intact and one by one the women returned to their homes. At the very edge of the village, near the place where we had entered it, there was a smoldering heap of ashes—all that remained of a house. A woman sat sobbing there on a pile of bricks, her head in her hands. Five little children huddled around her. The oldest, a girl of ten, held her baby sister in her arms and tried to console her mother. The other three

87

youngsters displayed the usual carefree attitude of children, scampering about in the ash pile or warming themselves at a small bonfire which they kept going by blowing on it. A small boy was brandishing a baked potato, which he had salvaged from the wreckage.

I approached the woman and spoke to her. She raised her head with a start. Her face was emaciated and grief-stricken.

"Was this your home?" I asked.

"Yes. But I haven't been living here for three months," she said in a low voice.

"Why not?"

"The Germans drove us out. My house was at the very edge of the village and that brought us bad luck. The Nazis set up a gun inside it to protect their position."

Piles of shell cases and mutilated German corpses were scattered amid the ruins of the house which the Nazis had turned into their main defense bastion. I recalled that our artillery barrage from across the river had been concentrated upon this very part of the village. The German battery stationed here and all its crew had been destroyed by a direct hit which caused their munitions supply to explode. In the course of this operation, the poor woman's house was completely wrecked, but that could not be helped—war is war. To effect our first river crossing we had dismantled several collective farmers' houses in order to build a pontoon bridge and get behind the enemy lines. This time the destruction of one house had made it possible for us to liberate an entire village from the Nazi gangsters.

"I realize you had to do it," said the woman through her tears, as though echoing my own thoughts. In her mind there was no doubt as to who was responsible for her wrecked home.

We took the woman and her children to the next house, where a few of our tankmen had gathered. Reassured by our soldiers, Alexandra Borisova told us her whole story. As she talked, the expression of hopeless grief on her face gave place to one of anger and determination.

For seven months she and her unfortunate family had suffered incredible hardships. Her husband was in the army. Of the five children with her, four were her own: Zena, aged ten; Valentina, aged seven; Tonya, five, and Vova, three. Sima, the fifth child, was a boy of eight whom she had adopted. Valentina had a bandage around her wounded right hand,

89

the result of a German bomb. After being driven out of her house, the mother and her four children had wandered about in the neighboring villages, living in earth huts in the woods. To feed her family she had to burrow in the snow and dig up grain that had been left in the fields. In the woods she met Sima, an abandoned orphan, and adopted him.

Sima, who had blond hair and beautiful hazel brown eyes, was now engaged in lively conversation with the tankmen, while dividing among the girls the baked potato he had salvaged. He, too, told us his story. His father had been killed in the Finnish campaign, and his mother had died in a Nazi air raid. He came from Staraya Russa, and his nearest relative was his maternal grandmother who lived in one of the neighboring towns.

"What's your grandmother's name, Sima?" I asked him.

"Granny."

"No, I mean her first and second names."

Sima just frowned in confusion. "Grandmother?" he mumbled in a low voice.

Our tankmen did everything they could to show their sympathy for Borisova. They shared their sugar, bread and tea with her children. They gave

90

her their word of honor that her house would be rebuilt. "We'll build it ourselves," said one of the tankmen.

We were already in the street when Sima came running after us bareheaded.

"Say, Uncle, can I be a tankman?" he asked eagerly.

"Of course you can," I said. "But you must wait till you grow up. They don't take them at your age."

"Oh, they'll take me," he replied. "All my uncles are in the Red Army."

"What uncles?" I said. "Why haven't you mentioned them before?"

"They're my mother's brothers: Uncle Lenya, Uncle Vanya, Uncle Vasya, Uncle Kirya and Uncle Andrusha."

"And their second names?"

"Timofeyev, all of them."

Now at last I knew the name of his grandmother. "All right, Sima," I said, "get ready to join the Red Army. But first we'll find your family."

❋   ❋   ❋

The Nazis had left the mark of their cruelty on the village. Konstantin Popov, a perfectly innocent

91

collective farmer, had been shot before the assembled population. Elizaveta Afanaseyeva was publicly flogged because her children had been found playing with cartridges they had picked up in the street. Now the Nazi gangsters had been driven out, and thousands of Soviet citizens had regained their freedom. Our tankists and infantrymen walked about proudly among their machines surrounded on all sides by the enthusiastic inhabitants. They looked with loathing at the German corpses that littered the village.

Some time later an official report listed the results of our battalion's work in the capture of Yuryevo. Here the most interesting figures are quoted: Germans killed—140. Material captured: 14 guns of various brands all in good condition; 93 automatic rifles; 297 ordinary rifles; 11 trench mortars; 7 anti-tank rifles; 60 trucks; 9 motorcycles; 39 horses; 3 station warehouses containing ammunition, army clothing and foodstuffs. In addition we wiped out the entire battalion headquarters of the 502nd Rifle Regiment, and seized all its documents.

Chapter VIII

THE MAMMOTHS ATTACK

Now THAT the last link of the enemy defense chain was broken, every minute was precious—it was essential to pursue him without interruption, not to give him a respite. But equally precious were every drop of fuel, every cartridge and shell, without which we could not advance.

Lack of supplies was holding us up. Our fuel tankers and ammunition trucks had not yet crossed the last river. Our men fretted with impatience.

. . . It was night when the supplies finally arrived. Our men were trained to do everything in the dark. Skilfully and quickly they set about refilling their tanks and munitions cases. Everyone tried to get as much as possible, to grab more than the others. Tankmen are never as greedy when they receive their rations of canned food, biscuits and sugar as when they replenish their ammunition. "What's the matter with you, do you begrudge me an extra shell for the Germans?" I heard Tank Commander Kali-nichev say in a hurt voice to the chief of supplies. The KV tank crews stocked their ammunition with extraordinary concentration as though they had never seen a shell before. They wanted to cram shells into their vest pockets, anywhere at all. Solovyov, Kalini-chev's gunner, stood with a shell in each arm, holding them like babies. He was perplexed—he had no space left for them. . . .

The tankmen were eager for a good hot fight.

Major Maximov assembled the commanders of the crews and explained the next task. The Germans had fled to the village of S. where they had appar-ently been reinforced by reserves. They were pre-paring to make a stand. This new defense line had to be broken and the enemy forced to resume his flight. Astakhov and his tanks were to remain in reserve during the first stage of the operation; they were to be used later—in the course of the battle it would become clear where the KV tanks could be thrown in with the best effect.

Shortly before daybreak the white Mammoth tanks and the baby tanks with white-hooded infantrymen and submachine gunners perched all over them went into battle. On an open field extending in front of the village, the Germans met us with a barrage from their anti-tank guns. The first explosions of enemy shells were our signal to deploy.

I followed the battle from the observation post of our infantry commander. A well-aimed shot from a German gun whipped off the turret of one of our small tanks in the van. The caterpillars of two others were disabled. Seeing the effectiveness of their battery the Germans intensified their mortar and machine-gun fire on our infantry. The men dropped for cover and the tanks fanned out over the field. The momentary confusion in our machines was too apparent not to be noticed by the enemy. As they surged forward drawing the infantry behind them, the Germans showered them with a hail of shells and mines in an attempt to isolate them from the infantry, and the fascist columns launched a counterattack.

Two green rockets soared into the air: the long-awaited signal calling the KV's into battle. Suddenly with a roar that shook the ground and the air, the giants emerged in deployed formation from the grove near the road. The Germans directed a tornado of shells upon them, but our land battleships relentlessly moved forward through the sea of fire.

Our infantry rallied. Behind the steel cover of the tanks that had outstripped them, they began to roll forward in waves. The white disk of the hatch on Astakhov's tank, which was advancing on the right flank, opened, and a red flag flashed three times. This message meant that the third tank was to break into the village.

The third tank, commanded by Lieutenant Chilikin, suddenly enveloped itself with dense black smoke. Rushing at full speed with the ease of a whippet, the land fortress headed straight for the enemy. Through my powerful binoculars I had an excellent view of the German artillerymen. Their guns fired salvo upon salvo and hit their mark, but the monster was invulnerable. Before their eyes it relentlessly moved forward. A few minutes later, it tore into the village, turned to the right, and began to smash the fascist anti-tank guns and their crews who were trying to escape into shallow ditches.

The thunder in front of us was no longer that of exploding enemy mines and shells, but that of our own tank guns battering at new enemy fire points. From time to time I could see Chilikin's machine

A tank-borne detachment starts out on a fighting operation. *(Sovfoto)*

Camouflaged infantry are carried behind tanks to advance lines. *(Sovfoto)*

A tank-borne detachment mounting the tanks in preparation for an at
tack. *(Sovfoto)*

Russian tank and camouflaged troops fighting for a village converted by
the Germans into a centre of resistance. *(Sovfoto)*

flashing amidst houses and trees. I could even distinguish the inscription, "Happy New Year." Our workers' greeting was finally reaching the fascists. Soon other tanks joined Chilikin's. They cut into the dispositions of the German infantry which only a few minutes before had been preparing to counterattack but which was being "ironed" out from both flanks. Those of the gangsters who had not fled in time were squeezed into the snow.

Fifteen minutes later, all five of the KV's were in the village playing havoc with the Nazis who were cornered in barns and attics. Another fifteen minutes, and the rest of us entered the recaptured village. The tanks continued the pursuit of the enemy who ran in terror toward the rear. In the next two villages the KV's met no resistance whatsoever—they made a real triumphal march, punctuated only by a few machine-gun salvos and rifle shots fired by our men as they wiped out a few stragglers who apparently were unable to move fast because of the loot they carried.

We advanced another fifteen kilometers. Our tanks were approaching a big inhabited place and a railroad junction. It was certain that the Germans would defend its approaches with particular stubbornness. Our scouts reported that the town was surrounded by a strong belt of anti-tank fortifications.

Astakhov was radiant after the engagement. "That was the real thing," he said with satisfaction. "I feel all refreshed." The commanders of the other tanks, Yefimov, Chilikin, Kalinichev and Gomozov, were just as jubilant. The crews opened the hatches as wide as they could to show the world their grimy but smiling faces and exchange a few sallies with their comrades.

"Gene!" Konstantinov shouted to Dormidontov at the top of his lungs, "Gene, tell us something about the Nazi illusions!"

"They had no illusions—only confusions!" Dormidontov punned amidst general laughter.

En route, the KV's received an important new assignment: to go around the village of L. in a pincer movement and, without engaging the enemy, to break through to a point five kilometers ahead, and seize the railway tracks and the main highway, along which the columns of German reinforcements were already moving. Major Maximov took his place in one of the KV's. Along with another tank commander, he was to attack the village from the left, while Astakhov, commanding the three remaining machines, was to take it from the right. They were to make a junction on the road beyond the village, in the enemy rear. The village itself was a continuous network of timbered dugouts, each provided with machine guns, large caliber mortars and cannon.

"A hard nut to crack. If we tried to take it by frontal assault we might break our teeth. The tankmen's idea was the right one," remarked the infantry commander as he observed the village from his post.

Maximov and Astakhov had suggested the plan of flanking the enemy. It was clear that seizing the two main enemy communication lines would be like cutting the main arteries in a living organism. To attain this objective it was worth while renouncing what seemed the most obvious step—blockading the village itself. This could be left to the rest of the battalion's tanks, in order to divert the enemy from the tanks moving around it.

From the very start the battle was one of the fiercest I have ever witnessed. While we thought of it only as a demonstration of what our tanks could do, the Germans, motivated by animal fear of our machines, made a last convulsive effort to bar our

99

way at any cost. The German anti-tank artillery put up real walls of fire. Their roaring shells exploded on the small open field almost within a yard of one another. But during this terrible artillery duel between tanks and anti-tank guns, the main action was taking place unnoticed by the Germans: our KV's were penetrating behind the enemy lines.

Soon they flashed out their first radio report: "Village outflanked, forging ahead." With the help of such signals and the regular reports to the infantry commanders, I was able to follow the development of the action. This is what happened:

Soon after the five KV's effected their junction on the road beyond the village, they were attacked by fire from enemy artillery stationed in a farm to the right. Our tankmen had not expected this. Major Maximov and Astakhov once again divided their forces: the Major moved forward with two tanks while the three under Astakhov concentrated on the enemy batteries which were trying to hinder our operation. A hot engagement followed. Having turned all their turrets to the right, our commanders fired salvo upon salvo on the enemy battery emplacements. "Forward!" signaled Astakhov, and the three KV's moved to wipe out the Germans. From small

100

ditches along the road, small groups of Nazi infantrymen rushed against our tanks, hurling rockets intended to blind our crews, while others dragged out heavy boxes of explosives. "No doubt the shock tank wreckers mentioned in the German instructions," thought our machine gunners. A few machine-gun salvos, and about half of the attackers were wiped out. But the rest continued to crawl toward the tanks. With a few well-aimed hand grenades, our tankmen finally got rid of all of the vermin. In the heat of battle, our men did not forget to help one another. When one of the Nazis managed to climb onto Astakhov's tank, Kalinichev's radio operator, Shishov, directed a machine-gun blast at him, so accurately that, in the words of the crew, the "Nazi was licked down off that tank as though by a cow's tongue." All this while, the three Mammoths moved forward at a furious pace squashing straggling fascists into the snow. At last, the German pillboxes were reached and crushed under the steel paws of our white monsters like so much tinderwood. Then they raced forward to catch up with the other two KV's.

Major Maximov was far ahead, perhaps even too far, having been carried away by his own impetus.

101

After crossing the railway tracks, his tanks raced forward seven kilometers along the highway, where the Germans were bringing up a regiment of motorized infantry. The fascists did not stop when they saw the approaching tanks, apparently taking them for their own in the distance.

"Turn to the left," Maximov commanded the second tank. As a result, the two tanks barricaded the highway. Our gun commanders did not have to be told what to do. While their tanks turned left, their turrets effected a ninety-degree right turn, pointing their guns at the enemy column. Nor was any order required to open a running artillery fire on the fascists who were scared out of their wits.

"We gave them the surprise of their lives," Maximov told me later. "When our first salvos blew up the vanguard trucks with their infantry, the Germans on the others were paralyzed, at a complete loss as to what to do. This was exactly what we wanted."

A few German trucks somehow managed to escape, but nine smashed cars remained on the field full of dead and wounded. In the meantime, Astakhov covered the railroad tracks and the highway and began a battle which lasted five hours without interruption. Not a single German train or truck managed to pass through. Thus, Gomozov's tank stood astride the tracks firing in both directions. Though the battle was successful, Gomozov was dissatisfied with the result. "What's wrong?" I asked him. "The battle wasn't as beautiful as it should have been," he said. "The best part of the affair miscarried. A fascist armored train advanced on me, and I, dumbbell that I am, was stuck on the tracks. I fired at him a few times. I don't know whether I hit one of his wheels or whether he got scared, but he withdrew and never reappeared. What a beautiful fight it would have been! A tank against an armored train! Will I ever get such an opportunity again?" he concluded mournfully.

Chilikin's tank returned with its hatches smudged and singed by exploded shells. I looked inside and the first thing that caught my eyes were dazzlingly white piles of gauze. Tank Commander Chilikin and his chief gunner Meshchanchikov had been wounded in the head by fragments of an enemy shell.

Kalinichev's tank particularly distinguished itself in the battle for the road, withstanding eighteen attacks from fascist anti-tank guns and infantry shock detachments. His skilful driver, Dormidontov, performed such dizzy pirouettes on the field that the fascist gunners never managed to get him in their gun sights. On his return to camp he surprised all his comrades by bringing in two men attached by straps to the exhaust pipes of his machine: one was a wounded Red Army man with only socks on his feet; the other was a fascist, also wounded and wearing large Russian felt boots. It turned out that during a lull in the fighting Dormidontov noticed a wounded Red soldier crawling on the snow in a clearing. No sooner had he made up his mind to leave his tank in order to help his comrade than a scrawny German emerged from the bushes and ran toward the wounded man. Dormidontov cried to the radio operator: "Shoot down the vermin!" But the "vermin" had already reached the wounded Red Army soldier and it was impossible to shoot without endangering the latter. Beside himself with fury, Dormidontov stepped on the gas. When he arrived upon the scene the fascist had managed to pull off the semi-conscious Russian's big gray felt boots and was now hastily putting them on his feet in place of his own ragged footwear. "Kolia, don't disappoint me, don't let that louse get away with it," Dormidontov cried to Shishkov. The radio operator waited until the fascist began to run back to his bushes. Then a resounding burst from his machine gun eloquently expressed the feelings of the crew. The gangster flopped down into the snow.

"Pick up our wounded man!" the tank commander ordered the assistant driver, Solovyov.

"And the German, too!" Dormidontov begged.

"What for?"

"He has our felt boots on him."

"All right, take him too."

The felt boots were duly returned to their rightful owner, Red Army man Nesterenko.

The tanks had brilliantly fulfilled their task of cutting the German communication lines. They were soon replaced by infantry which dug in. But despite their success, the tankmen were not happy. Lieutenant Astakhov, company commander, had failed to return from the battle. One thought was in everybody's mind: had he been killed? I evoked his handsome oblong face, with its stubborn forehead and light gray eyes. I went over all the course of our acquaintance: from the shop where he assembled his tank to the moment when he left for the attack. And Lena, his wife, how would she receive this terrible news? But nothing was known as yet. Astakhov, we told ourselves, was not the kind of man to be lost in this manner, without a trace.

Chapter IX

THE DEATH OF
COMMISSAR KHARCHENKO

THE FOLLOWING day it was decided that in the forthcoming battle Battalion Commissar Kharchenko would replace Astakhov, the missing commander of the KV tanks. This news spread with lightning speed among our men, who had been depressed by the disappearance of their beloved leader. "Good. The Commissar himself is going to command us," they commented with satisfaction. At once, the spirit of the crews rose high and preparations for the engagement were pushed forward with redoubled energy. Everyone knew what it meant to be led into battle by this brave officer, whose life story was known to all and was now being repeated among the crews.

"He can do everything in a tank, from driving to firing the guns."

"He commanded a tank company in Finland."

"That's where he earned the Order of the Red Star."

"He has received nine head wounds from shell splinters. Three of them haven't been removed yet. . . ."

Born in Konstantinovka, and formerly a mechanic in the Donbass, Commissar Kharchenko was thirty-five years old. But the grave wounds he had received in Finland had left their mark: his hair was completely gray, and deep wrinkles furrowed his face. Nevertheless, his blue eyes remained merry and with his cheeks reddened by the frost, he seemed rejuvenated. He had a real passion for everything connected with mechanics, for his shop, his motor, his tank.

A few days earlier, accompanied by Bushkov, his technical assistant, he had personally inspected every machine in the battalion, and had even found time to fix a phonograph for his hostess's daughter in the village where he was quartered. Now he was again going over the machines which were stripped for action. Only half an hour remained before the moment agreed upon for the attack. Kharchenko assembled all the crews around his tank.

"I am commanding your company. Do you all know that?" he asked in a hoarse voice.

"We know, we know, Comrade Commissar," replied the tankmen eagerly.

"Have you taken note of what I told you in the tanks?"

"We have."

"Have you repaired everything that had to be repaired?"

"Yes."

The Commissar proceeded to explain the company's task in the coming battle, and slightly raising his voice, concluded: "I want you to fight today three, four, no, ten times more fiercely than yesterday. In the first place, we must avenge Commander Astakhov and his brave crew. In the second place, we must kill no less than a hundred Fritzes for our two wounded comrades, Chilikin and Meshchanchikov. In the third place, comrades, do not forget that we are here not to amuse ourselves, but to destroy the fascist vermin, all of them, unless they surrender. You and your tanks have already scored glorious successes. For the sake of the magnificent workers who made these remarkable tanks, for the sake of all the workers and collective farmers who

108

sent us gifts, for the sake of Stalin, let us double our achievements.

"To your tanks, march!" Commissar Kharchenko commanded drily and himself got into Yefimov's machine.

When the Commissar urged the crews to fight for the sake of those who were working for them behind the lines, they recalled the day on which the gifts had been distributed and felt deeply moved. How much tenderness and love there was in the letters accompanying the packages! "Fight the fascists ruthlessly, fight with courage. We will soon come to help you," wrote two high school boys from the Ural. "All our hopes are in you, all our love and respect go to you," said a letter written in a childish hand at the dictation of an illiterate old collective farmer from the Cheliabin region. The old man, no doubt feeling that mere words were not enough to express his respect, added an original gift which happened to be allotted to Commissar Kharchenko. It was a big piece of frozen dough. Comrade Popov, shop fireman of the Cheliabin plant, told us that the old man's gift had at first been refused at the collection centre. He had then opened it to show what was inside. On New Year's Eve the Commissar

109

again opened it at the front in the presence of the tankmen. Inside the dough there was a roast duck, and inside the duck a pint of vodka. "Do you realize what this thing represents?" said Commissar Kharchenko on that occasion. "It shows a profound love, a loyalty which cannot be expressed in words. There is only one way of honoring such gifts—by victories at the front." Then he added more gaily: "As to the old farmer from the Ural, let him be assured that for each duck in aspic, there will be a hundred Nazis frozen to death."

The KV tanks went into battle. All day long they fought in the environs of a big inhabited place, wiping out the man-power of the enemy which tried several times to counterattack. The tankmen showed particular skill in "ironing" out the German infantry entrenched in the snow. The fascist riflemen and machine gunners had a hard time trying to escape from our onrushing tanks. They sank into the snow as into deep mud: no sooner did they get one leg out than the other stuck in, leaving them a helpless prey to our steel Mammoths whose mass of fifty tons pressed the fascist vermin through the layer of snow into the ground.

The Commissar's tank, led by our best driver,

Konstantinov, set the example. In the heat of the battle, a heavy German shell hit the tank's turret from the left, stunning and slightly wounding the gunner, Kustov, and the radio operator, Vedishchev. To keep up the barrage on the target, a big dugout, the Commissar himself sprang to the gun and with a few well-aimed shots silenced the German battery which obstructed our movement.

After the preliminary gun duel, the tanks supporting the infantry assaulted the strongly fortified enemy line. It was necessary to urge the infantrymen not to lag behind and to capture the enemy fortifications at any cost. Commissar Kharchenko opened the upper hatch of his tank and called out to the men: "Forward! Follow us, brave soldiers! Death to the fascist vermin!" As these inspiring words resounded over the field, one of the enemy shells crashed against the leading tank. The hatch was immediately slammed down, and the tank rushed forward. Seeing that their Commissar had begun the decisive assault, the infantrymen rushed behind the four powerful land battleships with a thunderous "Hurrah!" Twenty minutes later, the battle was over. Our tanks were moving unmolested along the German trenches and dugouts, while

111

our infantrymen used their bayonets to finish off the few resisting Nazis.

"That's the kind of tankmen we like!" the infantrymen expressed their enthusiasm about the bravery of their comrades during the lull that followed.

"That's the kind of infantrymen we like!" the tankmen returned the compliment.

"And what a wonderful Commissar! A real hero!" came from all sides. The operation of the two arms had in fact been perfect.

The tanks left the battlefield and returned to their assembly point for repairs and replenishing their fuel and ammunition. I noticed that the head tank moved slowly and drowsily, and that the Commissar's jovial face failed to appear above the open hatch. No one at headquarters liked the slow pace of the tank. "What's happened?" we cried out, unable to stand it any longer, and ran out to meet the machines. But our questions were drowned out in the roar of the motors, like the twitter of birds in a storm. The machines stopped and there was a moment of silence. From all the hatches tankmen emerged. They were removing their leather helmets, when the words of one of the commanders resounded sadly in the dusk: "Comrades! Our Commissar is dead." Our hearts stopped beating, tears glistened in many eyes. I saw men who had braved death crying like children.

Commissar Kharchenko was killed by a shell while he addressed the infantrymen from the open hatch urging them not to lag behind. The words "death to the fascist vermin" were his last ones. He was already dead when he led his men to the assault. They saw how the Commissar's snow-white tank rushed like a hurricane deep into the line of German fortifications smashing everything in its path. Inside the tank was Kharchenko's inanimate body, but he had come to life again in the spirit of his troops. Konstantinov realized that no one knew of the Commissar's death—that the men thought they were fighting under his leadership. Gritting his teeth, the driver hurled his machine bearing the body of the Commander into the most dangerous spots. The rest of the tanks followed, and their élan was so irresistible that soon only ruins were left of the German line.

The heroic Commissar was buried that evening. At his open grave, Battalion Commander Maximov urged his men to take ruthless revenge on the Germans for their beloved Commissar. "I have lost my

113

best assistant, the Commissar. But I am convinced that he succeeded in imparting some of his remarkable character to every one of you, and that you will prove this in the coming battles."

"I swear to emulate our Commissar!" driver Konstantinov stepped forward and pronounced these words in a stern and solemn voice.

A triple salvo was our last salute to the Commissar.

Chapter X

FORTY-EIGHT HOURS IN A BESIEGED TANK

Two days had passed since the disappearance of Astakhov and his machine, yet despite all our efforts not a trace of them could be found. "Is it possible that the Germans have disabled his tank and captured it?" we thought with consternation. We repeatedly sent out scouting parties, but each time the returning men just shook their heads when questioned.

The tankmen were disconsolate. Junior Driver Knutov was particularly upset about the loss of Astakhov. Each time he heard the negative reports of our searching parties, he went back to his machine, and leaning on the caterpillar tread, wept silently. His best friend, Leonid Kireev, was a member of Astakhov's crew. They had always been inseparable, and even when they wrote letters home, they used to do it together. I recalled that in the train to the front, the two friends shared a cot and always talked together until late at night.

That evening, Knutov upon his return from battle, stood as usual near his tank, absorbed in his grief. His comrades urged him to eat his supper—some excellent canned meat—but he obstinately refused. Suddenly new glad tidings, winged as a bird and stunning as a shell, spread over the camp: "Astakhov's crew is alive!" Knutov rushed to the command post, where many other tankmen had already assembled. Two members of Astakhov's crew, Predannikov and Tenditny, emaciated and blackened with soot, sat on a cot in front of the commander. Predannikov's hand was bandaged. This was their story: In the heat of the battle, Astakhov's tank had raced far ahead of the enemy flank and kept up an effective fire on the Nazi defenses. A heavy enemy shell smashed the tank's fore wheel, and sent it spinning. Seeing this, the Germans opened fire on it from all their batteries. For a full hour the thunderous crash of shells exploding against the tank armor deafened the crew. The motor and the gun were disabled. Astakhov could not signal for help, as he was hidden from the sight of

116

our troops by a grove. Finally the Germans ceased their artillery barrage and tried to rush the tank with almost a full battalion of men armed with hand grenades and dynamite sticks.

"Don't shoot until the enemy is within 100 meters!" Astakhov warned his crew. Our three machine guns, with their muzzles trained on the Germans, remained silent. The boys, eager to wipe out as many of the attackers as possible, counted every meter, every second. . . . Only when the first hand grenades began to fly at the tank, did they open fire from all three machine guns at once. The fascists dropped to the ground, but continued to crawl toward the tank. Our boys picked them off one by one. Several hours passed thus, the men in the tank trying to save their ammunition. Toward evening the Germans had retreated to a distance of some 200 meters. Astakhov ordered Kireev to make his way toward our troops and ask for help. Senior Sergeant Kireev took five hand grenades and cautiously opened the hatch. All around was silence. He glided down into the snow, and disappeared into the darkness.

Later that night the Germans continued to move small groups around the tank but avoided coming

117

close. The tankmen were surprised at this excessive caution—in the darkness the Germans had a better chance of setting the tank on fire or blowing it up with dynamite. What could be the fascists' design? the men wondered. Meanwhile night went by, day was beginning to break, and still Kireev had not returned nor was there any sign of help. Astakhov ordered Predannikov and Tenditny to try to obtain help. The two men tried to protest saying that they wanted to share his fate to the last, but Astakhov would not hear of this. Armed with hand grenades, and moving with infinite caution they crawled for two hundred meters to the grove, and from there raced to our lines.

Great as was the joy of the battalion at the discovery of the missing tank, Knutov could not share it fully. The fate of his friend Kireev was still unknown.

A three-man expedition, including Tenditny, was organized to reconnoiter the best possible route along which our towing machines could move to rescue the disabled tank, and to make their way to it with a sack of provisions for Astakhov and Makhalev who were still in it. Battalion Commander Major Maximov enclosed a little note to Astakhov congratulating him upon his conduct and promising speedy help. Senior Sergeant Knutov's request to be included in the rescue party was granted.

Our small expedition, however, was unable to bring help to the besieged men. The Germans opened a heavy fire every time they noticed the slightest sign of movement, barring the approach to the tank with machine guns and occasional shots from mine-throwers. Nevertheless, our men were able to observe that the Germans were engaged in some strange kind of engineering work around the crippled machine.

When morning came, however, the Nazi besiegers around the tank had vanished. Our commander smelled a rat, but decided to begin his rescue operations anyway. Forty-eight hours had passed since the tank had been encircled. And then, just as our towing machines were preparing to rush from the grove where they had been concealed, Astakhov himself suddenly appeared among us, as though he had sprung from the ground.

"Comrade Commander, where are you coming from?"

"From my tank."

"We are on our way there."

119

"You must not go near it."

"Why?"

"You'd be walking into a trap."

Astakhov then explained that all night long the Germans had been working around his machine mining all the approaches to it. They planned to blow up not the disabled tank but the machines that they expected to come to its rescue. To warn us he had sent the last remaining member of his crew, Makhalev. When he saw that we were about to start and that the Germans had withdrawn in order not to interfere with our intended movement, he decided to leave the tank. It was a hard thing for him to do, but it was necessary in order to save other tanks and the lives of his comrades. Taking one machine gun with him he arrived just in time to warn us of the danger. Makhalev followed him almost immediately. A special detail of sappers succeeded in salvaging the damaged machine. Thanks to the alertness and courage of Commander Astakhov the fascist design was foiled.

A few hours later, to the great joy of all the KV crews, and especially of Knutov, the last missing member of Astakhov's crew, Senior Sergeant Kireev, was picked up by a medical unit in the woods. He

These peaceful citizens are already in the shallow trench before the shooting. *(Sovfoto)*

Women removing bodies of relatives shot by the Germans who committed wholesale murder of the male population. *(Sovfoto)*

Russian families seeking their dead after the German retreat from their village. *(Sovfoto)*

Russian men and boys who might be of assistance to the returning Soviet troops were murdered by the Germans before their retreat. (Sovfoto)

Russian residents joyously welcome their Soviet liberators. (Sovfoto)

A bereaved father bends over the bodies of his wife, son and five-year old daughter tortured to death by the

Wholesale killing of Soviet citizens, with their backs to a trench, so their dead bodies will fall on those of their

had lost his way and had been wandering in No Man's Land for forty-eight hours.

While besieged by the enemy, Astakhov and his crew wiped out about a hundred Nazis. Before his machine was disabled, he crushed two fascist batteries and destroyed four of their strong points with his artillery fire. The rest of us had passed many nerve-racking hours of uncertainty over the fate of his heroic crew. Now they were together again sitting in a big hut on a tarpaulin spread over the floor, painstakingly cleaning the mechanisms of their guns. This was how I remembered them in the assembly department of the Ural plant. Then, too, they had sat greasing their guns and testing the different parts of their apparatus. "Well, how will the machine work?" the plant director who had dropped in for a while asked them. "Rest assured," they had replied. "Coming from you and operated by us, it will work wonders!" They certainly had kept their promise.

Chapter XI

FORWARD UNDER THE SOVIET FLAG

IN THE LIBERATED villages and towns, the first people to meet us were always the guerillas. While our infantry covered by tanks was busy breaking down the last points of resistance, with isolated groups of fascists still firing from attics and cellars, civilians sprang up among us as though from nowhere, with automatic rifles, machine guns and hand grenades. They were the local guerillas who always help the regular troops in the job of smoking out and destroying the remnants of the Nazi vermin. They are extremely valuable, for they know intimately every little street, cellar and basement and go about their work like professional exterminators smoking out vermin from every hiding place.

We had just cleaned up one village. Our Belanchevadze suddenly ran up to a group of guerillas whose rifles were still warm. "Shaterchik!" he cried to a young man in a black coat, who was issuing some instructions to his group.

The young man turned around and scrutinized Belanchevadze with a long questioning look. Suddenly his face lit up, he jumped forward and in a loud, childishly enthusiastic voice exclaimed: "Iliushka! Is it you?"

The friends embraced. They had studied together at the Moscow Technological Institute and called each other by their nicknames.

"So you are a guerilla, Shaterchik?" said Belanchevadze.

"Yes—I'm the commissar of our group. Let me introduce you—here is our commander."

"My name is Anatolii," said the commander, shaking hands with Belanchevadze. He was a small round-faced man, with the bearing of a soldier. A German automatic rifle was slung over his shoulders.

"Where have you been active?" asked Belanchevadze.

"Right here," said the commissar making a large circular gesture. "Don't you know we've been helping your advance?"

"You mean our tanks?"

"That's right, Tonia! Galia! Boris! Mitia!" cried the commissar, and keen-eyed guerillas, boys and girls, ran up to him. "These young people have just returned from a scouting trip behind the enemy lines. It is they who advised you on the route to follow."

We removed our gloves and heartily shook hands with our young friends. Three of them turned out to be "kinfolk" of our tankmen—former tractor drivers. As to Tonia, she was a seamstress in civilian life—now she was the best machine gunner of the group. "A real artist in 'stitching' the Germans!" said the commissar jestingly.

The guerillas gave us a brief account of their heroic exploits behind the enemy lines. Their first commander, Tomson, former manager of an oil refinery, had been killed in action. But this group avenged his death by killing hundreds of fascists. One guerilla, named G., burned a hut with 24 fascists who refused to surrender. Another, an elderly collective farmer, S., after the death of his commander, conceived the design of recovering his body and burying it. S. made his way into the village and found Tomson's body unburied near the German headquarters. He showered the German officers with hand grenades and taking advantage of their confusion drove away with the body on a sled. The beloved commander was buried in the woods with full military honors. A monument to the hero erected at his grave will soon replace the markings on the trees made by the guerillas.

In the village of Podborovye, liberated by us, I attended a common meeting of collective farmers and tankmen who elected a new Village Soviet. It took place in one of the houses that had escaped destruction by the Germans. I saw many of our countrymen who had spent more than three months under the yoke of the fascist vandals. Most of them were women. There were also a few old men and many children. The young and middle-aged men were at war, dealing blows at the fascists on the front with the regular army or from the rear—with the guerillas. As in pre-war times, a portrait of Stalin stood on the chairman's red-covered table. Political Instructor Shcherbak opened the proceedings. "By order of our Commander-in-Chief we have come here to drive out the German occupants, to liberate our towns and villages from the fascist yoke. We have fulfilled part of our task."

Before the election of deputies to the Village So-

viet, citizen Chebikin read the records of the atroci-
ties committed by the Nazis in Podborovye. His
voice resounded angrily in the frosty air: ". . . During the period of their rule the Germans burned 78
houses. They shot and hung 42 persons . . ."

Every name he read was engraved in our brains
in letters of fire; every one of them sank deep into
our very hearts. Hatred and desire for revenge
raged in every one of us, as the terrible list was
read. Our boys were unable to sit still, they clenched
their fists and their jaws, they could not suppress
their indignation. It seemed that if one more name
were read, they would rush toward their tanks
and fly once more into battle, to shoot, smash and
crush to death the hated executioners and gangsters,
to avenge the honor and lives of our Soviet citizens.

The feelings of our soldiers were somewhat softened when Red Army man Karpichev's wife began
to speak. Weeping with joy she thanked us from the
depth of her heart for the liberation of her village.
"We never lost the hope that it would be given to us
to see the world and you, our countrymen, once
more. We knew that we would be liberated. And
this is the man who liberated us. There he is!" she

exclaimed solemnly, pointing to the portrait of Stalin.

"It's true, isn't it?" said an old woman to a tank-man who was sitting beside her. "You came directly from him to our Podborovye, didn't you?"

The tankman, not without pride, of course said that Stalin himself had sent us here.

After the elections, the collective farmers wrote and signed a letter to Stalin. This moving docu-ment concluded with the following words: "Let our powerful Red Army live long and grow increas-ingly stronger. Let it ruthlessly fight our enemy day and night, in the sky and on earth, on water and under water!"

Chapter XII ·

A HEROIC NAME

All day long our units had fought with varying success. This was the final decisive attack intended to break through the main line of the enemy fortifications on this sector.

"Tankmen, don't disappoint us. Thousands of eyes will be looking at you from the ground and from the skies," Vershinin, the Commander of the Tank Troops, exhorted his men.

In the heat of the attack, when our head tanks with the infantrymen they carried were already breaking through the first line of enemy barbed-wire entanglements, a large group of enemy planes suddenly appeared flying out of the sun. Some were dive-bombers and some fighters, but they all carried bombs. The withering machine-gun fire of the fighters and the fragments of exploding bombs decimated the first rows of our attacking infantry and riflemen. A few more such strafing forays from fighter planes would have frustrated our attack.

Just at that moment, two of our own planes cut straight into the Nazi squadron. Like falcons descending upon a flock of crows, they pounced on the enemy, causing great confusion in his ranks. The whole sky seethed with the fire of guns and the roar of motors. The cloud of vultures forgot the ground —each of them was too busy looking out for his own skin. This relieved our infantry and tankmen who continued the attack on the enemy with increasing fury.

"It's burning! It's burning!" cried our soldiers from all sides. It was not clear at first whether this cry was joyful or alarmed. But then once again someone cried triumphantly: "It's burning!" and everyone saw the plane turn upside down in the air showing a swastika cross on one wing, and dive in a tail spin. Our own planes were turning the sky into a real hell for the fascists. Two more enemy planes, severely damaged, began painfully to move toward their own lines. One of our planes, too, was hit; without losing height it began to fly back to the airdrome.

"We've only one plane left, and there are still

seven of the scoundrels!" someone cried in alarm.

A mortal battle was taking place on the ground, at the very center of the enemy defense line. Our KV tanks, having levelled the Nazi barbed-wire entanglements, thus opening the way for our infantry, were now firing at the enemy strong points and anti-tank guns. From all sides resounded the mighty "Hurrah" of our men who had penetrated the main German fortifications.

Meanwhile, in the sky, there was the tragic spectacle of one plane fighting against seven. The Soviet falcon kept them busy for another few minutes. A joyful hurrah went up from below when he shot down another Messerschmitt. Suddenly the joyous exclamations broke off: our mortally wounded falcon began to fall faster and faster. . . . Thousands of eyes grew wide, thousands of hands thrust up in the air as though trying to catch the falling plane.

Our troops now had completely seized the so-called "impregnable" German main defense line. They were grateful to our flyers whose timely intervention had permitted attacking forces to complete their operation, but were saddened by the tragic end of our heroic fighter. One hour later they learned that the hero was Lieutenant Timur Mikhailovich Frunze, son of the famous Red Army general. The eyes of the tankmen, soldiers as war-like and fearless as Timur himself, filled with tears. We, soldiers and commanders of the KV tanks, lost in him not only a hero, but also a dear friend.

"Poor Tanya Frunze . . . back there in the factory . . . how will she survive this blow?" said Mechanic Knutov mournfully.

"She came with us to the station . . . and he accompanied us into battle . . ." said someone else with deep emotion.

Astakhov stood up and removed his black leather helmet from his head. The other tankmen, too, rose and bared their heads. Astakhov, speaking in a slow and solemn voice, took an oath to avenge Timur's death and to fight against the enemy as fearlessly as Timur and his father, Mikhail Vasilievich Frunze.

"We swear," his words were echoed by all present. Battalion Commissar Tkachenko suggested that we name one of our KV tanks in honor of our hero: Timur Frunze. Each crew begged that the name be given to their machine. It was finally decided that it would be given to the tank which most distinguished itself in the fight against the fascists. Thus began a competition for a glorious name.

Chapter XIII

STARAYA RUSSA

Two ancient cities, like two brothers, stand on two sides of blue Lake Ilmen: Staraya Russa and Novgorod. White wintry fields, snow-covered hills—this land has seen much during its many centuries of history. Here fought the free citizens of Novgorod, here flew their flags in many a bloody battle with foreign invaders. This past glory still seems to shine radiant amidst these fields. Old Russia! Great, invincible, eternally young!

This city of Staraya Russa was now in German hands. We could see it distinctly from our positions: our recent fifty-kilometer thrust across frozen Lake Ilmen and its tributaries, a real march through ice, blizzards and deep snows, had brought us close to the city, almost to its walls. Now our troops were busy "mopping up"—cleansing the surrounding villages

132

of fascists every day, incessantly, methodically. A considerable number of officers and soldiers belonging to the 90th and 30th German Divisions were "mopped up" in our Soviet villages, mopped up so radically that they will never see the light of day again. The Germans had also stationed here a division of their Elite Troop gangsters, the so-called "Death's Head" division—after each engagement with us, they fully deserved their name.

Out of the three hundred populated places in the Staraya Russa district, our infantry and tanks had now liberated more than half. Our ski detachments co-operating with the guerillas had cut many railroads and highways, German communication lines extending from the west to Staraya Russa. One of our ski detachments penetrated into a prisoners' camp situated on the city's outskirts and liberated several hundred soldiers and civilians.

The liberated prisoners brought a German camp guard with them. He sat before us, a scrawny fellow, unshaven, covered from top to bottom with an indefinable grayish crust.

"What is this crust from?"

"Pickle brine," one of the prisoners explained volubly. "He tried to hide from us in a barrel of dill pickles. . . . We pulled him out, and on the way here the brine froze on him."

Hearing the machine gun bursts from our ski battalion, the prisoners had staged a mutiny. They smashed the barracks doors and ran outside. The guards took to their heels. Some of them rushed to the commissary building and concealed themselves in barrels, empty or containing dill pickles. The prisoners, infuriated by months of German cruelties, pursued the guards and killed all of them, except the one who now sat before us, covered with frozen brine. He sat in a corner cringing and casting frightened glances at his captors. "He should say thank you for not having been pickled," our narrator concluded amidst general laughter.

One tale followed another—everyone wanted to relate his sufferings. There was, for instance, Nikita Voytov, a thinnish fellow with a hoarse voice, a long beard and moustache. He looked no less than forty. Actually he was a boy of twenty. In German captivity, men age five years each month. And aging is not the worst thing that can happen to them. Hundreds die of hunger and cold.

"In December," Voytov related, "the Nazis took a few hundred prisoners to work at Dno. The cold was ferocious. Half naked men were put on open freight cars. We told the interpreter that we'd surely freeze since we had practically nothing on us. He just laughed: 'You won't croak. It'll be easier to work without clothes. And if you do croak it won't be a great misfortune either.' The train left. Many of the men began to stiffen from the wind and frost. They collapsed, some dropping on the floor of the car, others out of it onto the ground. These were shot dead by the guards."

We cut many supply lines of the German garrison in Staraya Russa, and every day the Nazis' position and morale deteriorated. The guerillas played a great part in these operations. The small group which had been active in the district since the first days of the German invasion had now developed into several large detachments, among them the famous "Ivan the Terrible" unit, which inspired the Germans with an almost mystical awe. During one month alone, the guerillas in the city and the outskirts had destroyed 196 fascists, 23 trucks with ammunition and one staff car. They had also shot down a Nazi bomber and blown up three railroad bridges and two supply dumps. The civilian population of the district cooperated with the guerillas.

The city inhabitants and collective farmers have not bowed before the German invaders. When the fascists asked for volunteers to work in Germany for "six months," not a single man offered his services. The proponents of "voluntary" work then resorted to the whip. They forced men into labor gangs and sent them to Germany under guard. Many "volunteers" succeeded in making their escape and joined guerilla detachments.

In the city, the White Guard Bykov headed the municipal office located in a building next to the German Kommandantur.

"A scrawny fellow, red-headed, slobbering, wearing a brand-new suit," such was the portrait of the German-appointed "major" drawn by refugees from Staraya Russa.

"One day I went to see him, to ask him for medical aid," citizen Filippov related. "I explained that I had been hurt during an explosion. 'Where, in what explosion?' the Major asked me. I told him that a group of German gentlemen had been having a good time and had thrown hand grenades at the passers-by, just as a practical joke. A fragment from this bomb had hit me. 'What?' said the Major. 'You dare criticize the actions of their excellencies, the

German officers? Get the hell out of here!' All I could do was to lick my wounds like a dog. There is only one infirmary in the city, and you have to pay 10 marks for each treatment, while the highest wage under German occupation is 30 marks a month. . . ."

The Nazis closed all the schools in the city and the entire region. Under threat of execution by a firing squad they ordered the teachers to burn all the works of the Russian classic authors without exception. Later they added foreign and even German authors to the list of books to be burned. Special placards were posted stating that Staraya Russa was an ancient German city. In their efforts to give the city an authentic "German" aspect, the Nazis herded cattle into the beautiful ancient cathedral, hung the corpses of people they had tortured at the crossings of all the main streets, and opened houses of prostitution into which they forcibly dragged women and adolescent girls. Yes, all this did give the city a truly German aspect. . . .

To some extent, even the Nazis came to regret this "Germanization." They found out that during their occupation twenty per cent of all the women forced into the houses of prostitution under threat of immediate execution fell prey to venereal diseases.

137

The German authorities issued a special order on this subject. This order did not deny that the diseases had been brought in by German officers and soldiers. It contained an emphatic appeal to diseased members of the armed forces not to rape women. The motive for this surprising piece of humanitarianism was not, however, the authorities' concern for the population. "One diseased soldier may contaminate tens of others. . . ." The Nazis were only worried about themselves. As for the unfortunate women, they didn't give a hang.

One placard in the city declared that "the birth of a ninth child or a seventh son entitles the parents to choose Adolf Hitler or Reichsmarshal Hermann Goering as godfather." Beside the placard, in the street, the Nazis hanged Nilova and Boytsova, two pregnant women, and citizeness Prokofieva, who was the mother of four little children. These three women had not committed any crime—the Germans hanged them as a "warning." For the same reason, as a "warning," they shot citizen Smelov and left his two-year-old son to freeze in the street. The little boy was, however, picked up by guerillas who took him under their care. There is still no end to the executions and tortures. Everywhere, in streets and on squares, the corpses of hanged men and women swing in the frosty wind. Who were these unfortunates? What were their crimes? One tried to protect his wife from a German officer: to the gallows! Another was accused of being a guerilla merely because he happened to be in the vicinity when guerillas sniped at a German patrol: to the gallows!

Such is the life of the inhabitants of Staraya Russa. They hate the invaders and ardently look forward to the moment when the Red Flag will again fly over the city, when the traitors, torturers and executioners will receive the punishment they deserve, when every tear, every drop of innocent blood shed by them will be avenged.

Under the rule of the German plunderers, the city has been completely impoverished and reduced to starvation. There is no trace of stores and markets. The food ration is half a pound of bread, which is supposed to last several days. Sickness is spreading among the population. The Germans shoot those who fall ill with typhus or force them to cross the lines on foot, in order to contaminate the Soviet troops.

The civilians reply with acts of sabotage which cause great difficulties to the German armies. Not a day passes without some catastrophe or accident along the railroad tracks or at the stations. German barracks are set on fire. Recently, the four-story building housing the secret field police was consumed in flames with all its documents and fifty fascist beasts. Three times the Germans moved their Staraya Russa airfield—and each time Soviet planes spotted and destroyed it. The target had been pointed out by our friends on the ground, who also helped us to destroy three fuel dumps and one ammunition dump.

In the streets of the city, the refugees told us, one often sees groups of people in front of some German placard. When you come close you see posted beside the Nazi sheet an issue of the *Tribune*, the underground newspaper printed by the Staraya Russa regional committee of the Communist Party. When a German policeman approaches, the people direct their eyes to the German announcement, pretending that they are reading it. The Nazis try every method they know to destroy the distributors of the *Tribune*, and have even gone so far as to print their own announcements under the *Tribune* heading, hoping to recruit readers by this stratagem. But it does not work.

140

The military position of the Germans in Staraya Russa has steadily worsened. They are hammered from the ground and from the sky, from the front and from the rear. Under our repeated blows they have begun a gradual withdrawal westward, toward Lake Chud. On and around Lake Ilmen they have tasted many defeats. Now history is repeating itself on Lake Chud, where Alexander Nevsky once inflicted a terrible rout on the beastly Teutonic knights, the ancestors of the Nazis.

Chapter XIV

CONVERSATIONS MAN TO MAN

As a rule, to converse with the enemy, we use the convincing language of machine guns, rifles, mortars, and air bombs. However, every day, by broadcasts we hammer into the brains of the Nazis intoxicated with their initial successes the truth that unless they give up their intention of conquering the Soviet Union they will be exterminated to the last man by our troops. All our attacks open with a concert of artillery. Listening to this terrible music, contemplating the innumerable corpses and graves of their comrades, the German soldiers have begun to reflect upon their fate. The exploding shells make them eager to listen to the words of reason which we address to them. They pick up our propaganda leaflets and listen carefully to the loud-speakers installed in our trenches. Using one of these loud-speakers, our 7th Guard Division converses every day with the soldiers of the encircled 16th German Army Corps. German prisoners—Corporal Paul Hirmann and Privates Dürr and Fritz Blomm—speak to their comrades whose dugouts are only 200 yards away. They address their friends by name from a loud-speaker whose voice can be heard within a radius of several kilometers.

"*Achtung. Achtung.* Attention, attention. My friends, don't listen to the lying promises of your officers that you will be rescued soon. Yesterday we all had an opportunity to see how they carry out their 'rescue' operations. When things became too hot for your garrison, your Captain Myerdress simulated a wound on his left hand and ran away from you in a plane. And he is a cavalier of the Knight's Cross. You know very well that your garrison was captured by the Soviet troops. Those who did not surrender were killed. We surrendered and now we are the happiest men on earth. . . ."

Often, by order of an infuriated German officer, trench mortars open a barrage upon the loud-speaker. We are forced temporarily to interrupt our broadcasts and let the guns speak. . . . Then our bold and tireless radio men, after moving the "fire position" of the loud-speaker, resume their cherished task which is not without danger.

One night, after having driven around the encircled German 16th Army, I spoke to the Germans through our loud-speaker. Some time before I myself had been with a Russian army unit encircled by the Germans for an entire month, but now the tables were turned: we had made our way out of the encirclement, and surrounded the miserable but still stubbornly resisting garrisons of the Germans. "We are in a pot covered by a tight lid," is the way one soldier of the 16th Army described its position in a letter home.

I found myself in a cozy dugout on the firing line. We were exchanging occasional shots with the enemy with machine guns and trench mortars. Boydin, our radio technician, advised us to use the beloved German singer, Lily Marlen, to attract the attention of the Germans before my speech. One of her lyrical songs engraved on a record suddenly interrupted the brutal bark of the trench mortars with a high-pitched tender trill. As if by command, the German firing ceased. During the ensuing lull, the voice of the singer resounded with striking clarity. But suddenly, the song was replaced by the follow-

A hero greeting a group of young satellites. (Sovfoto)

KV tank field repairs at the front. (Sovfoto)

A duel between a Russian (foreground) and a German tank. *(Sovfoto*

Russian tank camouflaged with hay and snow. *(Sovfoto)*

ing announcement spoken in the purest German: "Attention, attention. Boydin informs the Germans that an officer who has arrived in the most powerful Soviet tanks from the Ural is about to address them."

The silence continued—that was the main thing. I read the German text, prepared in advance:

"Soldiers and officers of the encircled German army. You know your position better than I do, we won't discuss it, it is too sad a subject. We shall speak of more interesting subjects.

"I have come here with the powerful Soviet tanks that we manufacture in the Urals and that you have nicknamed 'Soviet Mammoths.' Our group covered the distance from the Urals to Staraya Russa—over two thousand kilometers—in two days. Not bad, is it?

"Our Mammoths joined battle with our troops. Thousands of shells were showered upon us. This was a real inferno, and for a moment we thought: have we traveled so fast only to hasten our death? And your artillery went on thundering and thundering. Every one of our tanks received several hits from your shells. But their armor proved so strong that not one of them has been put out of action, and

145

to this day they are all still fighting. You even succeeded in encircling the Commander of our Tank
Group, Lieutenant Astakhov, whose tank you temporarily disabled by a hit in its fore wheel. For
forty-eight hours you fired at him from all sides. He
replied in kind, but it seemed that he was doomed.
But you yourself know what happened: we managed to pull our tank out and save its crew, and on
the spot where it stood we gathered seventy corpses
of your comrades. Our tank crew of five men wiped
out seventy Germans—not a bad balance, is it?"

A short machine-gun burst suddenly interrupted
my speech. I thought that I would not be allowed to
proceed. *"Achtung, Achtung!"* cried Boydin at once.
"Our officer has not finished yet. One hour ago he
visited the headquarters of the Commander of your
290th Division, Major General von Lipp. . . . *Achtung, Achtung!"*

Again there was silence. I resumed my speech:
"Soldiers and officers. It is true that I paid a visit to
the headquarters of Major General von Lipp, Commander of your 290th Division. These headquarters
are situated in a dugout in the woods, but I assure
you, it cannot be compared to the dugouts where
you are now rotting. The general has six rooms with

hardwood floors. As I entered I slipped on the floor which was waxed and polished like a mirror, and barely avoided falling flat on my face. You are doubtless smiling when you think how I would describe your trenches where men slip and fall into deep stinking mire at every step. . . . You are right. Your trench is a less desirable place for visitors and even for its inhabitants, than the general's headquarters.

"In the general's dugout there is a piano—he enjoys good music. In this respect, however, you need not envy the general, for, as you know, we delight you every day with our artillery concerts. In one of the general's rooms there is a dazzlingly white enameled bathtub, which gave me the desire to undress and plunge into crystal-clear water, although I did not really need it, as we often have the opportunity of visiting our own bath houses. Then I thought of you. . . . How long ago is it since you took your last bath? And what linen the general has! Fragrant, smoothly ironed, with monograms. . . . Where is yours? According to a commissary order we captured, the last time you changed shirts was two months and six days ago. How revolting! What is the color and smell of your shirts now?

147

"In the general's dugout we discovered a stock of hundreds of bottles of champagne, burgundy, Cognac and vodka, all reserved for his personal use. What did you eat for dinner today? The general apparently thinks that wine does not go with your food, which consists exclusively of rotten horse meat.

"All this I have seen in your general's headquarters, recently captured by our troops. Among these troops were tank brigades from the Ural. The Soviet armies have more and more tanks, and the ring of fire around you is being drawn tighter and tighter. How can you escape?

"At the beginning of the war, you Germans addressed the same question to General Galitsky whom you had surrounded. I was with Galitsky's unit and I saw how he saved his men. Unlike some of your generals, he did not run away from the encirclement in a plane with a few of his intimates; he kept on fighting and escaped with three quarters of his division. But you won't succeed in escaping. In the first place the Soviet ring around you is too tightly drawn, and in the second place, able commanders, among them our old friend General

148

Galitsky, are in charge of the operations destined to annihilate you. Is it likely that he will let you slip out, having learned by experience what such encirclement means, and how to obstruct all possible means of escape? No, you will not succeed in breaking our ring. Do not sacrifice your lives in vain; surrender! At home, your wives, children, and friends await your return. You will be sent back to Germany after the war. . . .

"Goebbels has recently tried to amuse you by telling you that you were not encircled at all, that on the contrary you have encircled and annihilated our 7th Guards Division and killed its Commander Bedin. You must admit that both you and we were vastly surprised by this piece of news. You, because you know better than Goebbels who is really encircled and what is the real situation. We, because our 7th Division has never been destroyed, and is still fighting successfully. Only a few hours ago I spoke to Colonel Bedin, the commander of this division, who is in the best of health. The Colonel asked me to tell you, that although you have buried him in radio waves, he will bury you all in the ground, unless you surrender.

149

"Think it over, think it over. Follow the example of thousands of your comrades—surrender, surrender!"

"The broadcast is over!" announced our radio director. After an hour's lull, the battle flared up again.

Chapter XV

TANKS AGAINST TANKS

COLONEL KATENIN arrived at our battalion head-quarters. He was a squarely built, kind and resolute man, in a leather overcoat. Everyone knew the Colonel: the commanders who had long served with him in tank units and the tankmen with whom he had fought in recent battles.

"The Colonel is here, there must be something exciting ahead," was the unanimous opinion of the crews.

Katenin assembled the commanding staff in a grove. "The enemy," he announced, "has brought up tank reinforcement in our sector. He is preparing to effect a breakthrough to his encircled 16th Army Corps. Our assignment is to frustrate this manoeuvre, to join battle and to bar the way of the German tanks. . . ."

The faces of the tankmen gleamed with joy. They had long been looking forward to just that: pitting their strength against the enemy's tanks. It is true that the battalion had been incessantly fighting against enemy infantry, artillery, parachutists—but they had not yet encountered tanks, the much-praised German tanks.

The crews went about their preparations for the forthcoming tank battle as though it were a great holiday. But Senior Lieutenant Astakhov was unhappy: two of his five tanks were undergoing repairs, among them his own, of which the armor bore many dents from German shells. Astakhov and the crews of these two tanks were indignant and cursed the Germans for not having waited until their tanks were in shape. The Lieutenant was in a quandary. He thought it unfair to order one of the tank commanders under him to yield him his tank, but he also considered it an absolute disgrace not to take part in the battle. The battalion commander finally came to his rescue. "This is what I can do for you, Astakhov," he told the heart-broken tank commander, "you can direct the tank battle from the ground—from the observation post nearest the battlefield, that of the infantry commander."

152

Astakhov brightened. He recalled his past experience as an infantry lieutenant. He would know how to throw in his infantry at the best moment and place to support the tanks.

At five-thirty in the morning, under a dark blue sky with little flocks of silvery stars still gleaming and a full moon waning far to the west in the breaking light of the day, our tankmen who were stationed in a small clearing began warming up their machines. The air was pure and frosty, but there was already a taste of spring in it, and a smell of pine tar which the tankmen greedily inhaled. The machines were divided into groups, and each group had occupied the starting point for its operations. Everything was ready for the battle.

At five-thirty-five, the familiar whining drone of German bombing planes was heard from the west— the usual harbinger of an attack. The drone grew increasingly louder. Soon, an enormous flock of yellow-winged, black-bellied planes were above us. They deployed in a circular formation preparatory to diving. The cheerful morning stars seemed to go out as the black bodies of the Nazi vultures moved into the sky. One, two, three planes dived toward the edge of our woods. A dozen deafening explosions. . . . We awaited the next ones. But none came—and the diving planes vanished. A group of our fighters had suddenly attacked the gangsters of the air and forced them to withdraw. The sky, which only a few minutes ago had seemed covered by the silhouettes of the fascist Junker bombers, was now cleansed, and the last stars cheered us with their tender gleam.

From the command post came Colonel Katenin's order to advance a few hundred meters and prepare for our counterattack.

Our flyers prevented the fascists from carrying out the necessary "softening up" of the sector which they had chosen for their intended breakthrough. The German artillery now took up this task. Under cover of its fire, large masses of infantry moved toward our defense lines. The dull roar of tank motors could be heard amidst the rattle of machine guns and the explosions of shells. "Aha," said driver Konstantinov, "the German pigs are on the move. We'll roast them as soon as we're out."

By concentrating superior numbers the enemy succeeded in pressing back our troops in one sector and even in occupying a village, which, incidentally, was no longer a village except in name. All the

154

houses and buildings had been burned. But beside the village was a road junction through which the German troops could rush in order to develop their success. Colonel Katenin regarded this junction and the approaches to it as the most important sector, which was to be particularly watched by our tank-men.

Emerging from behind the German lines, six heavy and medium enemy tanks raced toward the village. "Time to attack," decided our colonel, and ordered Lukianov's group acting in cooperation with the infantry to advance toward the village and the enemy tanks.

A violent battle ensued. The Germans doggedly defended the positions they had just captured. Our machines were showered by an anti-tank trench mortar barrage. Groups of German infantrymen armed with hand grenades attacked them incessantly. But they failed to stop our advance. The battle now engulfed the village, and the German tanks stationed behind it seemed to hesitate before moving into the inferno.

"The bastards are waiting for an opportune moment," exclaimed Katenin and, turning to his signal man, commanded: "Tell Azobkov and Astakhov not

155

to be so nervous. Let them keep their shirts on. When the time comes to move, they'll be told."

With a thunderous "Hurrah" which resounded all over the battlefield, our riflemen battalions began to dislodge the enemy from the village at bayonet point. This was apparently what the fascist tanks had been waiting for: splitting into two groups, they smashed at the village, trying either to pinch it off or to break through to the road junction. Lukianov's tanks noticed this manoeuvre. They, too, split into two groups and rushed across the path of the Germans, opening a flanking fire on them as they moved. Two groups of three tanks each clashed with two enemy groups. Numerically, the opposing groups were even, but no sooner had the first shots been fired than our superiority was evident: two German tanks took fire on the move, two others had their treads damaged, and the remaining two took to their heels. We lost one machine.

"Well, so far we're holding our own," said Katenin with satisfaction.

A little later he repeated his praise, when the infantry commanders reported that the tanks had helped them to occupy the village, smashing nine German guns with their fire and caterpillars.

Meanwhile the battle raged. . . . Both sides incessantly attacked and counterattacked. At last, Astakhov reported: "Eight German tanks are trying to outflank us." From the command post the order was sent to Shliapnikov, the commander of the tank group: "Join battle."

Shliapnikov, too, had eight tanks. For a moment we thought that the next tank engagement like the first one earlier that day would be a clash of numerically equal forces. But Astakhov, whose information was excellent as a result of his close liaison with the infantry, warned us that at a distance of three miles to the west our scouts had noticed a large group of enemy tanks advancing toward the front. Katenin seemed worried. He hastily scanned his map, then cast a glance at the battlefield from his observation post. "Apparently they're sending their armored strength over in waves," he thought aloud. "Fine! We'll smash them in waves." He ordered Azobkov to attack the Germans on their flank as soon as the groups of eight joined the battle, while Astakhov was to obstruct the road and then throw in all his tanks to prevent the third German group from approaching.

The machines could not yet be seen, but the roar

of their motors grew louder every minute. Artillery fired, shells exploded. Suddenly all was confusion. On the top of one of the hills, eight German tanks emerged in a triangular formation, like a flock of cranes in the sky. Moving at top speed they attacked our infantry. But our own tanks rushed at them in a frontal assault. Every second, the distance between the two groups, which looked as though they were trying to ram each other, shrank perceptibly. Suddenly the Germans stopped and fired a general salvo at a distance of two hundred yards. This initiated a fierce tank battle. Amidst the smoke of firing guns and exhaust pipes which shrouded the battlefield, individual machines tried to manoeuvre. There was no way of distinguishing our own tanks from the Germans. Although only two groups were in combat their fight eclipsed every other action.

Colonel Katenin wanted to put the eight fascist tanks to flight as fast as possible. He did not doubt that we would eventually be victorious, but it was essential to complete this particular operation while Astakhov held the main German armor on the road that cut through the woods. Now we understood why the Colonel had ordered Azobkov's three KV tanks to emerge from their ambush. Our eight tanks were a

match for the enemy group of eight, but every minute was precious. The formidable Mammoths now
came down upon the German group. Four of the
enemy's tanks took fire and blazed like torches in
front of our attacking infantrymen who greeted this
victory with resounding hurrahs. The remaining
four enemy machines wheeled about and tried to
escape, but our shells overtook them and blew them
up. Two of our medium tanks were disabled, all the
rest were in condition to continue the battle. This
proved unnecessary, however. The sixteen German
tanks forming the enemy's third armored column
smashed headlong into Astakhov's covering force
comprising only three tanks. One of our KV giants
was commanded by Lieutenant Mashchev, former
gunner in the commissar's tank, who was substitut-
ing for Chilikin. "Your job will be to silence the
enemy's anti-tank guns," Astakhov had told him before the engagement. "Take up a position on the
road and keep firing at the German tanks. Die before you abandon this position."

While the tank fight raged behind Mashchev's
back, his anti-tank guns smote the leading machines
of the third German group which was trying to
break through to the battlefield. Disabled enemy

tanks obstructed the movement of his troops. The infuriated fascists sent up two anti-tank guns and directed them against Mashchev. But the KV, like a mighty fortress, stood firm and kept up a withering fire. The Germans tried to attack it with infantrymen, but two light tanks specially detailed to cover the KV dispersed these attackers.

A new salvo of anti-tank shells showered the heroic machine. Mechanic Knutov was deafened by a formidable explosion right next to his hatch. He looked through the slit and cried to the tank commander: "Stop firing! Our gun has been smashed!" One of the enemy shells had hit the barrel of the gun and bent it. If our tankmen had tried to fire it, the shell would have exploded in the muzzle destroying the whole tank and its crew.

"Too bad," thought the tank commander to himself. He continued to fire with his machine guns. Soon other tanks came to assist Mashchev. But now the Germans were reeling back from the battlefield. Aside from the gun, Mashchev's tank had three disabled wheels and dents in several dozen spots from direct hits by German shells. Some of the fragments were embedded in the powerful shell of the Soviet machine, but none had pierced it.

At a signal of alarm Russian troops return to their ambushed tank.
(Sovfoto)

Alighting from tanks in the theatre of war. *(Sovfoto)*

A tank-borne infantry detachment boarding the tanks for an operation. *(Sovfoto)*

"Comrades, Stalin says that to achieve final victory over the Germans we must eliminate their superiority in tanks and planes." *(Sovfoto)*

"Yes, brother, your case is serious," a tankman from another machine sympathized.

"A tank without its gun is not a tank, but a lifeless log," someone else commented.

The tank was out of action, it needed a thorough overhauling and a new gun. Mashchev kept up a stream of vigorous cursing at the Germans, as he walked around and around his tank, staring at its crippled gun barrel. Then he began to take some kind of measurements. He had apparently not given up hope of repairing the tank himself and making it once more fit for action. Everyone knew that Mashchev was as inventive as Dormidontov, and felt that he would surely think up some solution. Soon he stood before Company Commander Astakhov.

"Comrade Senior Lieutenant," he declared, "may I saw off 22 centimeters of the gun barrel? This will make it possible for us to fire the gun, and it won't be necessary to send the tank back to the factory."

Astakhov agreed at once. A former artilleryman, Mashchev had easily computed that even with its shortened barrel the gun could still hit the enemy at maximum distance. The tank was taken behind the lines. While the repair crew put new wheels on it Mashchev personally sawed off the damaged part

161

of the gun barrel. The tankmen worked for twelve hours without a pause. Soapy water was incessantly poured over the red hot saw. The men took turns resting and eating but the sawing was not interrupted for a minute. The following day, Mashchev's tank went into battle with the others of his group and kept firing at the fascists with its sawed-off gun. Its crew disabled two enemy tanks, one heavy and one light, and in addition wiped out many Germans. The enemy's attempt to break through to his encircled 16th Army cost him 2,500 dead.

Chapter XVI

"TROPHY" AND THE LOSS OF NO. 512

Our KV tanks tore into the village, amidst the crackle of rifles and machine guns and the explosions of hand grenades. Two or three houses in the centre of the village which the retiring Germans had set on fire, were blazing brightly. Huge flames dancing in the wind licked the heavy hoar-frost from the near-by poplars.

Speeding by the burning houses, Tank Commander Kalinichev thought for a second: "The Germans themselves should be in the place of these poplars so that the flames could kiss them till their eyes burst. . . ." Then the commander's gaze was once again directed forward along the smoking street, toward the alleys where certain stubborn Fritzes were still moving about and offering resistance. Now and then he commanded his driver, Dormidontov, to stop and send a shell into a stone

163

cellar where Germans were concealed, thus transforming it into their tomb.

The tanks raced about playing havoc with the
enemy. Excited by the battle the crews saw only the
German grenade throwers and anti-tank batteries—
targets to be hit and smashed relentlessly, without
mercy. . . . Suddenly, amidst this raging sea of fire
and death, driver Dormidontov noticed an enormous and beautiful dog, a pointer, rushing about
from house to house. As though he were being
baited he ran now into the empty houses, now to the
nests of the maddened Germans. "I'll make him
jump with his paws upwards," exclaimed machine-
gunner and radio operator Shishkov, taking aim.
"What's the matter with you?" cried Dormidontov,
giving Shishkov an angry poke in the ribs. "Are you
out of your mind? That's a dog, not a fascist."

Shishkov stopped, lowering his gun, and the rat-
tling burst that followed cut down two Nazi
grenade-throwers who happened just then to jump
out from behind a corner. "There are your dogs, you
can shoot them," said Dormidontov cheerfully, without taking his eyes off the observation slit.

The battle began to subside, but the copper-
coated dog still ran along the streets of the village

sniffing the corpses of the fallen Germans. He had lost his master.

Now the battle was over, the village was ours. At the first opportunity, Dormidontov asked the commander's permission to "get out to have a look at that dog." Twenty minutes later, at the entrance of the house where we were quartered, Dormidontov appeared with the great coppery dog who obediently followed him. The tankmen gave him a gay and noisy reception:

"Some prisoner you've got there, Eugene!"

"Here, 'Fritz,' here!"

"Sit up, 'Copper,' beg!"

The pure-bred pointer, despite his seemingly enormous strength, actually behaved as though he felt himself a prisoner. There was a frightened expression in his restless eyes. Apparently Dormidontov had managed to gain the dog's confidence, for the animal kept close to him and cast suspicious glances at the other tankmen. The driver stroked the dog and with a gesture invited him to sit down beside him. The pointer obediently lay down, but continued to show signs of fear. From time to time his satin-smooth nervous body shuddered and he turned his big head abruptly toward the noisy crew.

165

He kept his flappy ears close to his head and his enormous lips turned back to show his dazzling sharp white teeth. The well-fed creature shone from the tip of his ears to the tip of his tail.

"This is a German dog, boys," said Dormidontov. "Here's his number and description on his collar."

"He belongs to some officer, no doubt," said one of the boys.

"I suppose so," said Konstantinov. "His dirty dog of a master is lying somewhere in the gutter, while his noble dog is with us, sheltered from the cold."

Everybody laughed. "True, and it was I who saved his life," said Dormidontov. "Shishkov was about to kill him off with all the other dogs."

The tankmen cast reproachful glances at Shishkov. "You ought to be ashamed of yourself, Shishkov. Such a nice dog, and you took him for a fascist. . . ."

"And that's why I'm going to take care of this dog," Dormidontov went on. "The commander gave me permission to keep him in the battalion."

"Well, let's give him a name," said someone. From all sides came suggestions: "Fascist," "Gangster," "Adolf," "Hitler," "Goebbels," and so forth.

"None of these will do, boys," Dormidontov interrupted his friends. His eyes flashed gaily as he drawled in a mock reproachful tone: "Comrades, is it really proper to give such a name to a dog? Why insult an animal?"

His words were drowned out in a loud burst of laughter.

"Then what name shall we give him?" insisted the tankmen.

"Well," said Dormidontov, "we took the dog along with other German war materials. He's one of our trophies. Let's call him 'Trophy.' "

This suggestion was enthusiastically accepted.

Several months passed. Trophy became inseparable from the battalion. He quickly grew accustomed to his new name. He was particularly attached to Dormidontov, and when the jolly driver was away with his group, Trophy visibly missed him. All the tankmen became fond of the big pointer. They especially appreciated his good manners. He never bothered anyone for food until the regular meal hours. At dinner time, he accompanied his master to the field kitchen and ate what he was given out of a soldier's tin can. During the periods of Dormidontov's absence, Trophy walked alone to the kitchen and the cook fed him.

167

He richly deserved his daily bread. Trophy accompanied the tankmen on patrol duty, ran around the tanks, looked under them, made short excursions, sniffed and listened and tried to discover the presence of strangers. "A useful animal," was the tankmen's verdict.

One day someone teasingly remarked that the dog might someday take it into his head to run back to the German lines. Dormidontov took this warning seriously, and began to train the dog intensively. In a short time, Trophy learned to carry reports from headquarters to the tank group. He could also carry machine-gun ribbons and rifles.

"But you wouldn't dare to send him for your dinner," Dormidontov's comrades teased him. "He could never resist the temptation. He'd eat it up."

Trophy's attachment and fidelity to his master grew from day to day. On his way to battle, Dormidontov would take leave of the dog, shaking his paw, stroking him, giving him a lump of sugar. When all five tanks of the group returned from battle to the base, Trophy would jump up to meet them, always racing directly to Dormidontov's tank. "Trophy, old man, come here," Dormidontov would call from his hatch. In one bound, the dog would be

168

on the tank, sticking his nose into the opening and rubbing it against Dormidontov's helmet and his almost unrecognizable sooty face. One day, when his comrades reiterated their doubts as to the dog's ability to bring him his dinner, Dormidontov said firmly: "I'm going to send him. In ten minutes he will be back with my dinner pail." And he was right. The dog brought his meal intact. The tank-men were as enthusiastic as little children over this display of trustworthiness.

Meanwhile, the battles grew fiercer and fiercer. Dormidontov's tank sometimes was away for two or three days, and on such occasions Trophy was restless and worried. Several times he ran away to the front lines, but failing to find his master returned, gloomy and hungry. Only once did he succeed in breaking through to the battle line, during a violent tank fight. Our crews saw him running in confusion amidst violent explosions and careening tanks, and finally making his way toward the German lines. For five days he failed to appear. The boys thought that he had been killed or that he had returned to the Germans. But Dormidontov refused to believe that Trophy had betrayed him. He was so obviously depressed by the dog's disappearance, that his comrades, although their tongues itched with the desire to make jokes about a "deserting Trophy," refrained from doing so in order not to hurt his feelings.

Suddenly, the dog returned. He came back covered with mud and limping. His legs were bleeding from having waded through melting ice. "Poor Trophy," said Dormidontov, embracing his dog with tears in his eyes. Trophy only whimpered and wagged his tail, pressing himself close to his owner.

"Aha, you son of a bitch, so you did not like life with your old masters. You've come back as hungry as a German. Now you won't run away again."

"It's luck that those devils didn't eat him up," someone said.

A few days later, Trophy's wounds healed and he was ready once again to carry out every order of his master.

❋ ❋ ❋

One night, an urgent call came ordering all five of the KV tanks to go to our advance positions. The crews rushed to their machines, started the motors and waited for the command to go into battle. As usual, Dormidontov found time to say good-bye to his dog. The other members of the crew, Kalinichev,

Shishkov, Solovyov and Pisarev, also said kind words
to Trophy. The dog realized that they were his master's closest friends, and showed more regard for
them than for the other crews. By now Trophy was
known as the "sixth member" of Dormidontov's
crew.

The tanks were being sent up to prevent the Germans from recapturing a recently lost position on a
river. They had launched a powerful attack. After
two hours of fighting the enemy withdrew. The five
KV tanks fought like lions. Kalinichev's machine
which bore a large number 512 on its turret aroused
general admiration. Skilfully driven by Eugene Dormidontov, it executed the most difficult manoeuvres,
attacking the Germans from the flank and from the
rear. Its crew had long been famed for their skill in
smashing German guns and mortars, without dam-
aging their own caterpillars.

In this battle, too, Dormidontov cracked the German emplacements by sudden raids. His tank
smashed over a dozen German medium guns and
mortars. When the pursuit of the retreating enemy
began, he raced far ahead. . . .

After the battle, Kalinichev's tank driven by
Dormidontov failed to return. Trophy desperately

sniffed every other tank, but he could not find his master. Dormidontov had remained somewhere on the battlefield. As the hours went by the commanding officer and the returned crews grew more and more concerned over the fate of his tank. It could not be found anywhere in No Man's Land.

"They surely went too deep into the enemy lines, and were disabled," Senior Lieutenant Astakhov said gloomily.

Twelve hours passed, and still nothing was heard of Kalinichev's machine. A few scouts sent to reconnoiter as far as the German advance positions failed to discover any trace of it. Someone in the battalion suggested sending Trophy. "He'll recognize it from a distance, and the Nazis won't touch him because of the German badge on his collar," he said.

Early in the morning, before sunrise, Trophy was brought near a track made by one of the tanks and let loose. Apparently he had been waiting for just this moment. The intelligent animal bounded forward as though he understood clearly what was wanted of him. A few hours later, he returned to the assembling centre. He seized the first tankman he met by his overalls and began to drag him toward No Man's Land. "He's found them, he's found them," exclaimed the tankman admiringly.

Scouts Valin, Arovsky and Malchenko followed Trophy to the advance positions. The dog passed them and continued straight on toward the German lines, whence came bursts of rifle and machine-gun fire. It was dangerous to proceed, but Trophy moved stubbornly forward. If he advanced a few steps and saw that our men were not following him, he returned with an angry bark and tried to drag them after him. Our boys decided to move ahead cautiously. They crawled through the bushes, still led by the pointer. Suddenly the dog stopped, squatted, put his front paws on something black and turned his head toward the scouts. When they approached, they found the body of a Soviet tankman. It was Vanya Pisarev, Kalinichev's gunner.

"Poor Vanya, how did you get here?" whispered one of the scouts sadly. Pisarev's body was riddled with bullets. In his pockets there were some papers, the notebooks of all the crew. Apparently he had tried to make his way back to our lines to inform us of the position of his tank and had been killed by the Nazis while making the attempt. "Is the rest of the crew alive? Where are they?" the scouts wondered. They examined the notebooks found on Pisarev. But they found no answer to their question.

Among the papers was a large leatherette pocketbook belonging to Dormidontov. Trophy, who restlessly sniffed at every new object drawn out of Pisarev's overalls, suddenly jumped at this pocketbook and roaring fiercely ran on, heedless of the scouts who tried to call him back. He kept the precious object in his formidable jaws and, after making a few circles, rushed off toward the German lines.

"Where is he going? He must have lost his mind!" exclaimed Arovsky.

"Don't you see? He is surely following Pisarev's tracks. He'll find the tank now," said Malchenko confidently.

Our scouts took cover and decided to wait for developments, but a few minutes later they were noticed by the Germans who opened fire. They were forced to withdraw. An hour later, Trophy appeared with the same pocketbook in his jaw. He put it down in front of the scouts and stood as if petrified. The scouts opened the pocketbook and to their great joy found a fragment of a note signed by Kalinichev: ". . . Even a little bit. Maybe through Trophy. We are still alive. Using up the rest of our ammunition. Have killed about a hundred of the beasts. Will not surrender."

The tankmen remembered that Trophy had been trained to carry cartridges and rifles, as though Dormidontov had foreseen the present plight of his crew. The scouts got a machine-gun ribbon from the infantrymen, wrapped it up in a rag and put it in Trophy's jaw. The dog without hesitation raced in the direction of his own tracks.

The bold and intelligent pointer made three more trips with ammunition. We computed that the disabled tank was about three kilometers behind the enemy lines. From his third trip, Trophy returned with his skin singed in spots and with a note attached to his collar. "Dear comrades: Thanks to you and to Trophy. There's a dog for you! He helped us kill another four dozen of the bloody German dogs. Good-bye, boys! These are our last minutes. They're pouring gasoline over us. We are going to die, but we know that our country will win. Send our greetings to our families. We are dropping Trophy through the lower hatch. He will get through. Good-bye." The note was signed by Kalinichev, Dormidontov, Shishkov and Solovyov.

A week later we pushed the Germans back and occupied the place where tank No. 512 had been disabled. Both its caterpillars were smashed. The

175

Germans had poured gasoline over it and set it on fire. Thus perished the heroic crew of one of the KV tanks which traveled from the Ural to Staraya Russa, and with it Eugene Dormidontov, the favorite of the whole battalion.

Today, there rises like a black rock on the battlefield the steel tomb of the four heroic tankmen. Our soldiers often visit it. Baring their heads, they grieve for their fallen comrades and honor their exploits. On all these visits they are accompanied by Dormidontov's friend, Trophy, who is now the pet of all the tankmen.

Chapter XVII

THE SCHOOL OF COURAGE

Astakhov's company and the whole battalion not only fight but also teach others to fight. The high command on this front, in view of the special merits and the rich experience of Maximov's battalion, has chosen it to train drivers, radio operators, gunners and tank commanders belonging to the tank reserves. "The People's Commissar for War has entrusted you with the task of transforming new tank commanders and crews into seasoned fighters," Colonel Katenin declared to our battalion commander. "However, you will still take part in the daily battles."

To teach others. . . . Yet not so long ago the tankmen of this battalion were considered inexperienced. I recalled their first meeting with Major Segeda and his stories about the various methods of destroying the Nazis.

177

"And if our tank is disabled?" one of the tankmen had timidly asked the Major.

"Repair it at once."

"And if the firing continues?"

"You must make repairs under fire and return to the fray."

"But supposing I'm wounded!"

"Ah, my friend," smiled Segeda looking at the young tankman, "in war one is sometimes even killed. . . . That's the way it is. Hadn't you heard?" The men laughed.

Less than six months had passed since that conversation. The young tankmen are now seasoned veterans. We have recaptured many miles and populated centres from the enemy, and many scars have been inflicted on our machines. Some of Lieutenant Astakhov's best men have been killed during these months; others, like Chilikin, Kononov and Mashchev have been seriously wounded. And the battles continue without respite, and the number of each tank's exploits constantly increases. They have accounted for hundreds and thousands of the invaders, and large numbers of crushed or crippled enemy guns, tanks and pillboxes. The fires of the war have forged the company into hard, fearless masters of their job, capable of teaching others.

The drivers, artillerymen, radio operators and tank commanders who arrived at our battalion for a course of intensive training were happy to learn that they would be under the command of Astakhov, whose exploits were now famous all over the front. Astakhov's first meeting with his new pupils took place in a friendly atmosphere. He knew that the tankmen sent to him had either lost their tanks, mostly old models, in battle, or had escaped from enemy encirclement and fought as riflemen.

"What was your job and on what kind of machine?" he asked Sergeant Vershinin.

"I was a driver-mechanic." Vershinin proceeded to list a few makes of tanks which he had driven into battle.

"And what kind of fighting have you been doing lately?"

The tankman was somewhat embarrassed, but continued to answer firmly: "I was in the infantry, Comrade Senior Lieutenant. First I served as a rifleman, later as a trench mortar gunner. At Klin I was wounded in the leg."

179

"Fine, now you'll be driving a machine again and what a machine!"

"Thank you, Comrade Senior Lieutenant. Many thanks. I hope it will be soon. . . ."

Junior Sergeant Gut had had similar experiences. After having been a tankman, he was an infantry scout and later a tank wrecker. Others had been liaison men, trench mortar gunners, artillerymen. They all spoke with emotion of their service in these branches, but did not conceal the fact that "their hearts beat with envy and longing whenever they saw a tank." They had the souls of tankmen, and no sooner did they arrive in the battalion than they rushed to the machines, staying in and around them till late at night.

After their talk with Astakhov, the new tankmen asked him to show them the machines of his company, and above all his personal tank in which, they knew, he had been besieged by the Germans for two days. This time it was Astakhov's turn to be embarrassed: his tank was under repair and had not taken part in the latest battles. "But some day I'll give you a real show with it," he promised.

He conducted his training course with great energy. His "pupils" were enthusiastic over the new

A liberated farmer and his family converse with Russian soldiers.
(Sovfoto)

The indomitable Russian people return to their villages to join in driving
the enemy from their beloved soil. (Sovfoto)

Automatic riflemen going into battle against the Nazis, a British "little brother" in the background. *(Radiophoto)*

Repairing KV tanks at the front. *(Sovfoto)*

machines, and often, when they had gone through a tank—Astakhov made them enter it through the upper hatch and leave it through the driver's hatch after a thorough inspection—they spontaneously expressed their admiration for the Ural workers who had constructed the new machines. The program of instruction included driving, mechanics, shooting, and finally fighting in a real battle. The pupils who were victorious received regular appointments as crew members.

Senior Driver Konstantinov was in charge of repairs. One day, Lieutenant Yefimov's KV tank returned from battle seriously damaged by a thermite shell, which had dislodged the turret from its base. The crew was unharmed, but the turret was bent, and it was impossible to use its gun. To repair this injury it was necessary to remove the turret and recast part of the armor plate.

"We shall repair the tank ourselves, and the boys will learn a valuable lesson," declared Maximov, the commander of the battalion. Yefimov's crew, together with the trainees, went to work. The battalion had no crane of its own. Two mighty oaks from the neighboring woods were used to hoist and suspend the turret which weighed many tons. The

181

tankmen themselves skilfully filled in the breach in the armor. A few days later, the tank was back in action. For this feat Yefimov's crew was cited in an order of the battalion commander. When the students congratulated Yefimov, he declared: "Athough the battalion commander did not mention you, you must thank yourselves, because now you will have a tank on which to train and to pass your examination."

Astakhov himself, sometimes assisted by infantry and tank commanders, directed the course in tactics and cooperation with the infantry. One day, he ordered his pupils to arm themselves with hand grenades and automatic rifles. "We're going into battle," he said. "A lesson in tactics. The Germans have brought up new tanks. Let us see how our machines handle them."

Commanded by Astakhov, the group of tankmen arrived at the front positions during the night and entrenched themselves near the post of the regimental commander.

By morning the action began. The Germans had prepared a counterattack which was to be supported with tanks and aviation. After a preliminary bombing, Nazi infantry and tanks assaulted our trenches.

182

They were met by a barrage of fire from machine guns and heavy batteries. "Keep your eye on the tanks," Astakhov kept warning his men. Part of the German armor assaulting our positions was at once put out of action by our anti-tank guns. The remaining machines engaged in duels with nine of our tanks that rushed out of the woods to meet them. The battlefield was covered with smoke. The first casualties occurred. Astakhov at the command post ordered his tankmen to bandage the wounded and keep hand grenades and automatic rifles ready. From that moment on, he became in fact the aide of the regimental commander who was leading our troops. When our liaison junction, a few yards from the commander, was hit, Astakhov ordered a few of his men to help restore it and organized the circular defense of the command post. Everyone forgot that he had come here for "training" purposes. This was a real and savage fight.

Suddenly, Major Pavlov, the regimental commander, groaned with pain. Both his legs had been hit by bullets. Calling for stretchers and bandages, Astakhov himself tended the wounds of the major and five other officers and sent them to the rear—what he had learned from his wife Lena, an army

183

nurse, proved extremely useful. For an entire hour Astakhov substituted for the commander directing the battle, until he had restored liaison and called out substitutes for the commanders put out of action.

Our troops repulsed the Nazis' counterattack, passed over to the attack and continued their advance westward.

Later in the day, the tankmen visited the battlefield, where four fascist machines turned by us into tombs had been abandoned. Two of our own disabled tanks were surrounded by their bustling crews. The "pupils" and the "teachers" became acquainted with each other.

"Want some help?" the trainees asked the veterans.

"No, thanks, we're almost through. We're about to leave. You'd better try resurrecting those Germans," driver Trofimov cried to them from his hatch.

The trainees made a thorough inspection of the German machines, examined the places where they had been pierced by our shells and memorized the most vulnerable parts of their armor. The following day, other groups of trainees came to study them. The graveyard of the fascist tanks was noted in our school schedule under the modest title of "field trip No. 6." We all hoped that there would be many such "field trips" in the future.

*　*　*

One day, guest tanks appeared in our battalion. Oval in shape, low to the ground, their motors deeply hidden inside their armored interiors, they made little noise. These tanks came from abroad. Assigned to fighting units, in the first battles they seemed to behave in a nonchalant fashion as though they were mere tourists on the battlefield. Their crews were entirely Russian.

"When will our 'little brothers' show the stuff they're made of?" the tankmen asked each other with impatience. They were referring to the guest tanks which they called by the caressing name of "little brothers." They had been sent us by our ally, Great Britain, and our Soviet tankmen, who had not yet had time to familiarize themselves with the new machines, handled them with extreme caution.

But a few days later it was impossible to say which of the tanks fought more bravely and more fiercely—our own or the British. Toward the beginning of spring, a battle took place with units of the

185

encircled German 16th Army. The day before, the KV crews had inquired of their commanders: "Will our 'little brothers' fight this time, too?"

"They certainly will, in every group," said Kordov, Commander of the British Tank Group.

About fifty tanks were concentrated in a wood, ready to be thrown into the fight. Only a few days before, this wood had not been much of a cover. Now it was all green. The tank ambuscade was perfectly concealed by small pine trees and the mighty branches of firs. Where did all this come from? "Spring, no doubt," the German observers must have thought as they watched the woods through their field glasses.

From the distance came a hum, which was soon distinguished as a mighty roar of several motors. Our bombers, the *stormoviks*, were going into battle. Accompanying Soviet fighters and wearing the same five-pointed stars, flew oblong British-made Hurricanes.

"It's a joy to see them working together in the sky," Tankman Krugly said enthusiastically.

"Soon, we, too, will start moving. And we'll work together just as well as they," said Driver Granatkin.

From the enemy's lines came the sounds of the

186

first bomb explosions, followed by the rattle of machine guns. Two green rockets soared into the sky—the signal for the tanks to attack. The steel wave of armor rolled out.

The Germans resisted stubbornly. Their anti-tank shells covered every yard of the ground over which our machines raced toward them. Close behind our KV tanks, which German shells can damage about as much as a shower of peas can hurt a stone wall, came the "little brothers," the British-made tanks. Their main task was ahead—for the moment it was essential for all of us to reach the enemy lines unharmed.

One KV and one "Britisher," commanded by Kordov himself, separated to the right in order to assault a huge strong point. Suddenly, out of nowhere, German planes appeared overhead, diving straight at the tanks. They aimed at the larger one, and soon bombs exploded near the KV, showering it with hot metal splinters and earth. Kordov's tank moved aside from its leader. Its upper hatch opened, and the barrel of a machine gun emerged from the opening directing a stream of tracer bullets at the enemy planes. The air gangster, having failed to hit the KV, began to attack the tank firing at him. Soon

187

the plane spent its supply of bombs, and tried to hit the tank with its gun, but without effect. As soon as he levelled out in the sky for a dive, the tank jumped forward or to one side. After having dodged the plane seven times, Kordov was apparently fed up with the whole thing. "Don't move this time," he ordered his crew when the fascist plane prepared for an eighth attack. "Fire point blank."

The roaring Nazi dive bomber now anticipated victory. But a ribbon of tracer bullets hit its motor. A sharp explosion, and a gigantic flame soared upward covering half the sky. The plane dropped out of the line of its dive, turned over and roared downwards wrapped in fire. The British tank, commanded by a Russian officer, won the duel with the Nazi plane and gave a most instructive "lesson" to our trainees.

＊　　＊　　＊

Later, when spring came, in a town where we were quartered, a group of workers addressed the following request to the tankmen: "The Germans have sullied our main square by burying their dead there. We are now digging them up to clean out the place. But the ground is still frozen. Your sappers

New KV tanks as they arrived at one sector of the front. (*Sovfoto*)

Camouflaged tanks speeding to the front. (Sovfoto)

helped us to blow it up. We need your machines now to drag away the lumps."

"We are always glad to clean our earth of this dirt," said Astakhov with a smile. Our mighty tugs pulled out and dragged away immense lumps of earth with fascists frozen in them.

THE END